Praise

The very first time I met Marja I was totally captivated by the way she was just herself to the core, unencumbered by other people's expectations and opinions, and the way she shone in her own strength has always stayed with me. I know that this book will challenge you, and make you smile... while giving you permission and courage to live the way you were designed, and not simply to live up to others expectations. Marja's honesty and generosity simply define her and her family, and their belief in people's potential truly has lifted the lives of countless thousands to dream big, and live life to the full. Thanks Marja for sharing your journey, and to every reader I say, be encouraged, read on, and be prepared to have your thinking enlarged, your capacity challenged, and your dreams given wings to truly fly.

>With much much love, Darlene Zschech

Marja Barnett is one of the most amazing, vibrant authentic women I know. Besides partnering with her husband Tommy Barnett to build a strong local Church she has positioned her children well and they are each examples of ministry legacy. I am thrilled that she has put pen to paper to pass on her wisdom. You will enjoy this window into her life and glean insight as you turn each page.

Lisa Bevere
Author & Speaker
Kissed the Girls, Fight Like A Girl
Messenger International

More than just her story, Marja's life is one of the most remarkable and inspiring accounts of a unique journey with God that every single person can relate to, and most people will relate to it on several different levels. You'll be changed, challenged and charged to become what God wants you to be—no matter what you have been, or are going through. I know that if you are honest with yourself before God, you will be a much better person for learning about hope and trust in God from Marja's life—it's my privilege to have watched it unfold—to God be the glory!

Tommy Barnett

Through Every Season

Through Every Season
with Marja Barnett

Margot Ah Kuoi

Tate Publishing & *Enterprises*

Through Every Season
Copyright © 2009 by Margot Ah Kuoi. All rights reserved.

No part of this publication may be reproduced, stored in a retrieval system or transmitted in any way by any means, electronic, mechanical, photocopy, recording or otherwise without the prior permission of the author except as provided by USA copyright law.

The opinions expressed by the author are not necessarily those of Tate Publishing, LLC.

Published by Tate Publishing & Enterprises, LLC
127 E. Trade Center Terrace | Mustang, Oklahoma 73064 USA
1.888.361.9473 | www.tatepublishing.com

Tate Publishing is committed to excellence in the publishing industry. The company reflects the philosophy established by the founders, based on Psalm 68:11,
"The Lord gave the word and great was the company of those who published it."

Book design copyright © 2009 by Tate Publishing, LLC. All rights reserved.
Cover design by Amber Lee
Interior design by Joey Garrett

Published in the United States of America

ISBN: 978-1-60696-401-9
1. Biography & Autobiography / Religious
2. Religion / Christian Life / General
09.01.21

Acknowledgements

To my husband Fred, who cooked, cleaned and did all the things necessary to make things "function" at home, while I wrote this book. You're the best! And to my children, Danielle, Joshua and Madeleine & my son-in-law Mark... I love you guys. Thanks for all your support.

Also, to my dear friends Jeanne Lueders and Cheryl Markel, whom I believe were sent by the Lord to help me. Thank you for giving your gifts so freely, and for the many hours you spent editing, listening and encouraging me... I couldn't have done it without you both!

Praise the Lord for his perfect timing, his infinite wisdom, and his unfailing love!

To my mother-in-law Joy Barnett, who was always there for me with her words of wisdom, inspiration and encouragement. By the grace of God, I was able to read this book to her during our Thanksgiving visit a month before she went to be with the Lord in December, 2007.

Earlier on that year, Joy told me of a vision she had of me coming from turmoil, out of a cocoon, to become a beautiful butterfly. What she shared that day not only confirmed how I had been feeling inside, but also strengthened and prepared me for her subsequent passing.

I was privileged to have been the recipient of years of wisdom, gathered first hand by a woman who lived her life selflessly serving her husband and family. I can still hear her soft, tender voice saying, "Show me the Pastor's wife, and I'll tell you about the Pastor."

I miss her greatly. Joy was more than my mother-in-law; she was my dear friend. I couldn't have made it without her.

Marja Barnett

Reference material:
Lynn Lane
Jo Lummer
"Portraits of Vision" by Pastor Tommy Barnett
Celebrating 20 years with Pastor and Marja Barnett

"Reflections of Joy" by Joy Barnett
"The church that never sleeps" by Matthew Barnett
Picture - Des Moines Sunday Register February 20, 1977
24 TwentyFOUR, A Legacy of Changing Lives, "A Time to Pray"

Photography:
Mark Knoles
John Madiol

Photos:
Phoenix First Assembly of God
The Barnett Family
Friends of the family.

From the Author

Margot Ah Kuoi

Rather than talk about who I am, I want to show you who God says I am!

It was August 15th, 2007, a day that would otherwise go unnoticed...a day of no special significance...or so I thought.

In the days preceding, I found myself questioning my seemingly ritualistic morning treks to the Prayer Pavilion to pray for an hour, asking the Lord "what difference is this making in my life, or for that matter, the Kingdom of God?"

I was about to realize just what a huge difference spending time alone with Him actually made. With no distractions, confusion or another soul in sight, the Lord had been preparing my heart to recognize His voice.

On this morning, after lifting Pastor Tommy in prayer and speaking a blessing over Marja, I heard the Lord say, "I want you to tell her story." Just like that! At the time, what He told me to do was more of a surprise than the fact that He had actually spoken to me.

Although it was something I would never have

thought myself capable of doing, any thoughts of fear or doubt were completely overshadowed by the overwhelming sense of assurance in my heart that I *could do* what He was asking of me. All I had to do was say "yes!"

By that same evening, I was sharing the events of the morning with Marja, and she was telling me of how her son, Matthew, had declared just the day before "Your story will be told."

Within the week, Marja and I were sitting in a local Starbucks, excitedly recalling memories of past events in her life.

Before embarking on this journey with Marja, mostly what I knew of her life, was gained from the stories and accounts told from the pulpit by Pastor Barnett. However, in just five, four hour meetings over coffee and lunch, that all changed. The Lord brought us together, knowing that our life experiences had been incredibly similar in many instances, enabling me to relate to her story on a very personal level. To this end, it was one revelation after another, as we laughed, cried, and reflected on how truly amazing her life has been.

Incredibly, five months later, the book was completed!

I say all this in the hope that you will be encouraged to do what the Lord has told you.

He's waiting to give you wisdom, finances and people to help you. He is everything you need to complete the task ahead, and the rewarder of those who earnestly seek Him.

He says I am an author. I trust, believe and obey Him, and so I have told Marja's story. To God be the Glory.

Table of Contents

Introduction: Searching for Significance 15

My Name is Marja (MAR-jah). 19

The Red-Faced Evangelist 33

My New Role as Wife 49

The Beginning of a Legacy. 63

Stand and Be Counted 103

This Place, This Time, This People 113

Timing is Everything. 133

Girlfriends 153

The Fruit of Faithfulness 179

Team Barnett. 199

Behind every great man, there is a great woman... and behind them both is an even greater God.

Searching for Significance

"For I know the plans I have for you declares the Lord. Plans to prosper you and not to harm you, plans to give you a hope and a future." (Jeremiah 29:11, NIV)

Writing this book has been one of the most wonderful, fulfilling experiences of my life.

To be able to sit down and recall years filled with memories, and reflect on how the hand of God has moved through every season of my life has been incredible. I have a deep sense of gratitude in my heart, that I'm not sure would have been possible had I not gone through this amazing process.

I now realize that long before I knew it even existed in God's Word, I innately understood the meaning of Jeremiah 29:11. For so many years, this basic principle; that God is real and that he has a plan for my life, was in fact, all I had to hold on to.

For years I struggled, searching for my own significance in so many areas of my life, not recognizing that I was significant to him by the simple action of responding to his voice and obeying his Word. I didn't realize that my childlike faith and trust in him was all he desired of me and that he would do the rest.

The Lord never professed that following him would be easy. In fact, he tells us that the road is narrow: yet, many give up on their marriages so easily at the first sign of trial and opposition, forgetting the covenant they made with the Almighty God.

Being married to a great man like my husband has not come without its challenges, but I am so thankful that we decided back in 1965 to make our marriage work, no matter what the obstacles. This was the turning point in our marriage, setting the tone for how our lives would be lived for the Glory of God. At that point, we placed our feelings and personal agendas aside, recognizing that God had indeed brought us together to fulfill his purpose and that there was a greater plan in place for our lives.

It's a very sobering thought to consider that many of the great things that have been achieved through my husband's ministry, may not even exist today had we not been aware of God's purpose, first and foremost, for us as a couple. There may never have been a Kristie, Luke, or Matthew, serving the Lord with all their hearts. Phoenix First Assembly of God, the Los Angeles, Phoenix and New York City Dream Centers, may not be standing as they are today, strong and proud, boasting to the world of what the Lord is doing.

Great men of God like Bishop TD Jakes, Jentzen Franklin, Coach Bill McCartney of Promise Keepers and Pastor Charles Nieman, all of whom were inspired to "dream again" at our Annual Pastors and Leaders

Introduction

School, may not have fulfilled their full potential in God had it not been for our complete, unified surrender to God's greater call on our lives.

My prayer is that as you read this book, you will be encouraged and inspired to be the best that you can be for yourself, your family, and for Jesus.

My Name is Marja

(MAR-jah)

I remember being a little girl, holding a small crucifix and praying to the Lord to guide me and give me direction.

In 1941, a time when the eyes of the world were on Europe watching Adolf Hitler's every move, a young eighteen year old girl named Irmalin, pregnant with her first child, was about to open a letter that would change the course of her life forever.

Just a few months earlier, her husband had left to serve his country in the war and fearing that he was not going to make it home, had written her this letter. Bloodstained and crumpled, it was now being delivered to her by the local priest.

She opened it apprehensively, afraid of what she might read inside. Sensing the importance of the message her husband was trying to convey to her, she read each word slowly, carefully. Somewhere within the letter expressing his deep love for her, and the regret he had in his heart that they may never see each other again, he told her that he hoped the baby she was carrying would be a girl. He then asked her to name her Marja if it was. I was born in Helsinki, Finland on December 4th, 1941 and my mother named me Marja Kaarina Makelaa.

When my mother finally received the news that my father had, in fact, been killed, she was absolutely devastated. With the exception of her alcoholic mother, whom she cared for, and her newborn baby, she was now completely alone. It was going to be tough, but she was left with no choice other than to raise me the best she could on her own... not a very promising prospect for a young girl at any time, let alone in the middle of a world war.

As the war continued to ravage Finland, with the constant threat of bombings and lack of basic resources, we were forced to eat from garbage cans to survive and live in the cellar of a house. After a time, even the garbage cans didn't supply us with enough to live on and my mother was forced to make some tough decisions. She began working on the streets as a prostitute to keep us alive.

I grew up quickly and learned to fend for myself. But, even at a very early age, I somehow always knew to turn to God for the things that I couldn't do on my own. I don't know how I knew, I just did. I clearly remember a real turning point in my faith as a small child, when one time, suffering from a really sore stomach, I prayed with my small crucifix in hand for the Lord to heal me, and he did. Up until this point, God had just been someone that I talked to, but this was the first time that I knew he had heard my prayer. I knew that he was real and that he cared about me.

As the years passed by, and with no end to the war in sight, it became increasingly hard for my mother to care for me. She knew that if I stayed with her in Finland, I would more than likely die from malnutrition, as I was very thin and suffered from stomach pains and dysentery. When I was three years old, she made another difficult decision and sent me to Sweden with thousands of other children in the same position as myself.

I was moved from hospital to hospital, seven in total. People from the hospitals said that I was a very angry child, pulling the eyes off dolls and preferring to keep to myself. Nobody wanted to adopt me because I was so mean, and each time I was left behind at the orphanage, the angrier and meaner I seemed to become. I was just a little girl… what did I understand of war and poverty? All I knew was that I had been sent to a far away place, I was all alone, and that I missed my mother!

In 1948, with the war over, my mother asked for me to be sent back to Finland to be with her again. She had always kept track of where I was during the years we were apart, and now that she had her life back together, she felt it was time for us to be reunited again. I was six years old when I arrived back in Finland, but I had very little memory of my mother and my life prior to leaving three years earlier. What was once familiar was now all very strange to me. Still, she was my mother and I was happy to be with her, but it was going to take time to adjust to being out of the orphanage and in a home again.

During the time that I had been away, my mother had married a man who was an alcoholic and was very abusive towards her. I vividly remember one time, screaming that I wanted to go back to Sweden after seeing him try to attack her with an axe. No child should have to witness such a horrible thing. It was very painful to see someone I loved being hurt, knowing there was absolutely nothing I could do to help or protect her. I remember being overwhelmed by an incredible feeling of helplessness.

A year after my return to Finland, my mother made yet another difficult decision; to send me back to Sweden a second time. Despite her best efforts to balance her life between me and her abusive husband, she just couldn't get past the deep fear that she would not be able to give me what I needed if I remained with her in Finland. I know this was an incredibly hard decision for her to make, because to this day, she still has trouble forgiving herself completely for sending me away.

On my return to Sweden at the age of seven, I was adopted by the most loving couple in their late 50s, Mr. and Mrs. Nils Holstrom. They had one son and loved me as their own immediately. They fulfilled the need inside me to be loved unconditionally and completely. My mother kept in touch with me through them, which helped me settle in with my new family. I continued to suffer from stomach pains and dysentery for many years, often struggling to keep weight on my small body.

My adoptive mother told me one memory she had of those early years was of me sitting chewing on a small bone, unable to stomach any of the turkey dinner that she had prepared for the family. The doctors prescribed nerve pills for me, perhaps thinking that the trauma of the war and leaving my mother were the real cause of my stomach problems, but she wouldn't let me take them. She also recalls many times when I would have to be brought home from school screaming and suffering from panic attacks, possibly sparked by memories of the bomb attacks during the war back in Finland. As time passed, the panic attacks became less and less frequent. I was able to lead a normal life and eat without the extreme negative reactions to food that I had suffered from in my earlier years.

I loved both of my new parents very much, but I was definitely "Daddy's girl." Each night after a long day at work, he would scoop me up into his arms and lift me up so high, which I loved and always looked forward to. I'm not sure if I felt betrayed or rejected by my real mother at that time, but whatever the reason was, I didn't want any woman to touch me, just him. He alone made me feel safe, secure, and assured that everything was going to be all right.

My new mom was a believer and raised me in the Lutheran faith. My dad was an atheist and even though he was the kindest, most loving man that I knew, I often wondered why he didn't believe in God the way I did.

I always felt a sense of closeness and peace whenever I prayed, and I knew for sure that God was with me.

My friends made fun of me for believing in God, but I always knew, even as a child, that he was real and that I was destined for something great.

My dad was the Fire Chief in Malmo, Sweden and we lived above the fire station, with all the other firemen living downstairs. As a young girl, I ran errands for the firemen on my bike to earn some pocket money. My half brother and I loved to join them during their recreational time and learned to play ping pong, a game which I still love to play today. I have always been very competitive, possibly a trait that I picked up way back then, playing games with my dad and other men twenty years older than myself. Those were happy days for me, filled with wonderful adventures and experiences with my best friends, the firemen.

I attended Kommunala Flickskolan, an all girls private school where I showed a special aptitude for languages, learning to speak English, French and German. I think it was at this time that I also started to develop my sense of style and dressing well. I loved to wear the little blue velvet beret which was part of our school uniform.

As I got older, my interests started to change. At sixteen, my mom enrolled me in gymnastics, as well as cooking and sewing classes, but instead of going to them, I would go on dates with boys. When she found out, my mother was furious and grounded me every Saturday for months. Right up until the age of eighteen my curfew was 11:00 p.m; although I always ended up sneaking in around 2:30 a.m. My dad knew, but never told my mom. He would always say to me, "just don't do it again," but I couldn't help myself; boys were so much more fun than studying.

In 1958, I was nominated to enter the Miss Sweden competition. My mother didn't want me to do it, fearing it would cause me to become even more distracted from my schoolwork than I already was. She was already having trouble keeping me focused on my studies, without a beauty pageant filling my head with all sorts of dreams and far fetched ideas. It sounded like so much fun to me, and I really wanted to do it. In the end, however, I gave up my aspirations to become a beauty queen and decided to trust and obey my parents.

At seventeen, I got a job as the secretary to the Chief of Police. I had always liked the idea of being a policewoman, and just loved being in this environment, even if it was only as a secretary. After work, I would go out in the cars with the policemen to pick up "bad guys." Over time, I came to realize that what I loved more than the actual police work itself were the city lights at night, and being around people. It was all very exciting, new and fun. I loved to have fun!

I decided to explore a new career opportunity which seemed better suited to my personality, and applied for a position as a stewardess with Scandinavian Airlines. The airline was very specific about what they wanted their stewardesses to be like. Applicants were required to be fluent in five languages and have reached a high level of scholastic achievement just to be considered. But more importantly, they needed to have the right "look." The stewardesses were expected be model types and could not weigh more than 120 lbs. or be less than 5'5" tall; it was all about presenting the right image. I was so excited when I was accepted immediately, but just as I was about to start my training, things around me started to change, making the prospect of traveling all over the world a lot less appealing!

My adoptive dad had always been very loving toward me, but I found it very hard to totally trust men my own age. I always had a lot of boyfriends, but I never really "liked" any of them. Perhaps it was because I always compared my relationships with them to that of mine with my father, or maybe it was because of what I had seen happen to my mother at the hand of her husband back in Finland. Whatever the reason, my perspective of men changed completely when I met Anders.

He was different. Anders made me feel safe and secure just like my father had. He was from a very affluent Swedish family and would often send me flowers and always treated me with respect. We loved to go dancing at night clubs and went as often as twice a week. When I was eighteen we became engaged, but even though I loved him very much, we would always get into arguments about God. He would say that God didn't exist and I would try to reason with him and explain why I believed that he did. It was always a sore point between us and caused a lot of problems in our relationship. Once again, as with my father, I couldn't understand why it was so difficult for him to accept that God was real. I used to think to myself, *If only he believed in God the same way that I do, everything would be so much better.*

The countries in Europe are very close to each other, so it was easy for my friends and me to get around. We thought nothing of going to another country just for the fun of it! At twenty, I went to Germany with some friends, just to go dancing. That is my nature; fun-loving and adventurous. It was during this trip, one night on a dance floor, that I was approached by a hairdresser who asked where I was from, and whether I would be interested in doing some modeling for hairstylists. I was flattered. It sounded like something new and fun; so when I returned to Sweden, I started to freelance as a hair model.

At a photo shoot I met another model, Birgitta, who became one of my closest friends. One day, out of the blue, I said to her, "Why don't we go to America? We could become movie stars." Just like that, the dream was birthed. I believed that this was it. I was finally going in the right direction; towards the greatness I had always felt was deep inside me despite all my circumstances. I was going to be a movie star!

We had heard that Americans liked to hire Swedish girls to be their nannies and decided that this would be a good way to get a foot in the door to our new careers. Anders, my fiancé, wasn't very happy with my idea, but I told him it would only be for three months and that the time would pass quickly. We could be married as soon as I got back. We'd already been engaged for two years; surely waiting another few months wouldn't make a difference, would it?

My parents were also against me leaving, afraid that I would marry an American and not come back. I assured them that I was in love with Anders; of course I would be back! As confident as I felt that this was the right step, I still felt the need to pray. I knelt down beneath my small crucifix hanging on the wall of my bedroom and prayed that the Lord would guide my steps and give me direction. This was a big step I was about to take, but I knew that whatever happened, God had heard my prayers and he would be with me.

Reluctantly, my mother paid for my airfare. It was August of 1964 when Birgitta and I boarded the plane for the United States of America. We were all decked out and definitely looked the part of movie stars; me in my white suit, big pink picture hat, pink sandals and Birgitta in her tight navy suit. We both had long cigarette holders in hand. We told everyone on the plane of our dream to become movie stars. I guessed by the way they reacted that they'd probably heard it all before, but I didn't care.

I knew I was different; I was going to make it. I was twenty-two years old... I could do anything!

Upon arrival in Los Angeles, we were each picked up in separate limousines and taken to our respective new families to work as nannies. It was all very exciting and new! The house where I was to live was amazing. I had never seen anything like it before in my life. That first night, the couple threw a huge party and I came out in my bikini to join them... what was I thinking? My new employer (the lady of the house, whom I'd just met), immediately pulled me aside and told me that my dress, or lack of it, was not appropriate for the occasion. I'd seen a pool outside and thought it was very appropriate, but I changed my clothes nevertheless.

She and I didn't get off to a very good start and from then on it was all downhill. She was mean to me, making me work on my days off and do things that weren't in my contract, like cleaning. The children were very spoiled, and I found communicating with them difficult due to my limited knowledge of the English language, which made things seem even worse. It was not as easy as I thought it would be. Still, I held on to my dream of becoming a movie star, with no real idea of how this was going to happen.

The Red-Faced Evangelist

This was my first impression of the young man behind the pulpit. I whispered to my friend "Why is he screaming and banging his fist so hard... and why is his face so red? Is he mad at people?"

A new friend whom I had met just a week after arriving in the United States invited me to a church meeting in Palo Alto, California, where she had heard a fresh, young evangelist would be preaching. This was my first experience of church in America. I had been raised a Lutheran in Sweden, which was nothing like what I was about to experience this night. The young man, Tommy Barnett, talked so fast I couldn't understand him at all, but I remember thinking how sincere and passionate he sounded about everything.

Something drew me back to church the second night. Now I understand that it was the Holy Spirit, but at the time, I felt that there was something at that meeting that was the answer to the prayer that I had prayed back in Sweden, asking the Lord to guide me and give me direction. When the young man gave the altar call, asking if anyone would like to receive Jesus as their savior, I went forward and he came down from the platform and prayed with me. I'm sure that he had never seen anyone who looked like me at any of his meetings before; yet I was completely unaware of just how much I stood out from the crowd, with my platinum blonde hair, false eyelashes, mini skirt and high heels. All I knew was that for whatever reason he was calling people forward, it was also for me!

Straight after the meeting I couldn't wait to get outside to light up a cigarette, but when I did something was missing, it didn't taste the same. Just one puff made my stomach turn and I felt like I was going to vomit. What was happening to me? I couldn't even stand the smell of the cigarette. A doctor back in Sweden had told me that if I didn't quit smoking, it was going to kill me. I would cough all the time, but I was young and of course didn't care that the cigarettes may be the cause of my problems. It was cool and I liked it, but this time something was different, I had lost all desire to smoke.

The young preacher found me outside and insisted on taking me home afterwards. We sat outside my house, where he continued to explain to me more about who Jesus was until four in the morning. It was difficult for both of us with the language barrier, but with his animated style and my limited English, I finally got the message. I remember there being a bright light all around us. It was, without a doubt, the most beautiful night of my life, the night I met Jesus and my husband for the first time.

In the days that followed, we went on many dates. He would pick me up in his fancy black Thunderbird, always pulling out of the driveway very fast to impress me. He had the most beautiful blue eyes, and the most lovely, soft hands that I had ever seen. We would sometimes drive thirty minutes to San Francisco just to have dinner, barely saying a word to each other, and not even noticing. It was so romantic; words weren't even necessary as we learned that love has its own language, and we both knew how to speak it.

I kept wondering when he was going to kiss me, and couldn't understand why it was taking him so long. All the boys that I'd dated back in Sweden couldn't wait to kiss me! He was different. He was interested in me, not my lips. However, as the weeks passed I began to think there was something wrong with me... was it my breath? He finally kissed me on our tenth date—not that I was counting! When I thought about it, being a preacher, he probably hadn't kissed many girls before. Our first kiss was sweet, and worth the wait.

To my disappointment, we never went dancing on any of our dates, and I could never understand why not. I loved to dance; maybe he just didn't like to or know how to! As time went on I found out that a lot of things that I loved to do were contrary to the ways of this exciting young man who had come into my life.

Tommy left California to continue speaking at more revival meetings. During the next couple of months we didn't see each other at all, but he did write the most beautiful love letters to me from all over the country. I didn't know how to respond to all this attention, as I had only just met him and didn't really know anything about him. It had been fun going out with him, but I certainly hadn't had time to think seriously about how I felt about him. So I never wrote back. He knew that I was engaged, but didn't seem to be concerned about the fact that I had a fiancé back in Sweden. He had one focus; winning me for himself.

One night I got a call from him in Canada. He asked if I was going to be home, and said that he had something very important to ask me. There was a strange urgency in his voice as he said that he would be coming to California as soon as he could. The very next day he was standing in front of me, proposing, and I was saying "yes."

In spite of the fact that I had said yes, I was still extremely confused about what was happening and the speed at which everything was moving. I felt totally out of control. I was thousands of miles away from my home, my family, and my fiancé, facing the daily challenge of the language barrier, and now I had said I would marry a man that I had only known for three months!

What had happened to the dream of being a movie star? Could a movie star be married to a man of God? I was also struggling with my feelings because I was still in love with Anders, so I wrote Tommy a letter saying that I didn't think that I could live his kind of lifestyle; it looked so boring and I was a party girl. I was used to dancing and having fun; there didn't seem to be any of that in the church. The next letter that I received from him was three pages long and all it said was "I love you," over and over again, and, "please marry me."

Tommy was so persistent and passionate... I remember thinking to myself, *maybe this is the guy for me* and for the first time since arriving in this country, I felt an indescribable peace come over me. This just felt right. In Tommy I saw everything that had been missing in Anders and all my former boyfriends. This man loved God more than I did and was not afraid to share it with the world. Because he loved God so much, I just knew that his love for me would be genuine.

So I wrote a "Dear John" letter to Anders, telling him that I would not be coming back to Sweden. Something incredible had happened to me, but I knew that even if I tried to explain it to him, he would never understand. So, I simply told him that I had to follow my heart and do what I now felt was right for me. I never heard from Anders again. I was scared and excited at the same time as I began to prepare myself to marry the man who had made such a huge impact on me in such a short time. I was now certain that he was the reason that the Lord had brought me to this country; Tommy Barnett was the one for me.

My new fiancé's background and mine were worlds apart, not just geographically, but also foundationally. He was raised in a stable, Godly home, the son of a Pastor. He gave his life to the Lord at the tender age of four, after hearing a message preached by his father about eternity, and how you would either spend it with God in heaven or without him in hell. On their way home from church, little Tommy insisted on making sure that he was saved, because he didn't want to miss going to heaven. He couldn't wait until they arrived home to pray, he had to make sure then. So, in the back seat of their car, as his father continued to drive, and with his mother by his side, he prayed the prayer of salvation with them. Finally, he was at peace, in his heart knowing for sure that one day he was going to heaven to be with God for eternity, and that was all that mattered to him.

Tommy began to preach at the age of sixteen years old when his father sent him as a substitute to a revival meeting in his uncle's church in Seminole, Texas. His father had presented him to his uncle as "the chip off the old block." His uncle was unimpressed. He wanted the block, not the chip! Still, once he got to Texas, Tommy's uncle realized that there was something special about this boy. He had an energetic, charismatic quality about him. He would sing, and play his accordion and trombone to draw in the crowds. Actually, the first time I saw him play the accordion I thought he looked so corny and just wanted him to stop wobbling around, sit down, and play the piano instead. I'm so glad that he didn't listen to me, as the people loved the way he played his accordion.

Even though our upbringings were so different, we did have one thing in common that I now recognize as being one of the key factors that has held our marriage together over the years. We both had, and still have, a childlike faith in a God who is greater than both of us. It was this childlike faith that would prove to keep us together through the tough times that were ahead.

Marriage is challenging for any newlyweds, but when you add a language barrier, cultural differences and different upbringings to the mix, that's a recipe for disaster... except in God's Kingdom. Being the wife of a young evangelist, who has a vision for his life all mapped out, would mean leaving my dreams behind to follow him. Deep down I knew that I was making the right decision.

There was so much to learn about this new life that I was about to begin. Without knowing that I was still struggling with my decision to marry him and become a preacher's wife, Tommy decided that it would be a good idea to send me to live with his parents in Kansas City. He called to tell them that he had met me and fallen in love, but was afraid that I may not be able to handle the life of ministry, as I was a new convert. He wanted me to experience firsthand what I was getting myself into, and believed that if anyone could model the life of ministry to me, his parents could.

So in October of 1964, I was on my way to Kansas City, leaving the bright lights of California behind me. I had never met his parents before and upon arrival at the airport, we only found each other because of the description that he had given them of me. To my surprise, they wasted no time whisking me straight off to church where they were practicing for their Christmas pageant, complete with a "singing Christmas tree." The choir was actually singing in a huge, man made Christmas tree!

I met so many people all at once, all wanting to shake my hand, hug me and talk to me. I know they were only trying to make me feel welcome, but I felt completely overwhelmed. Once again, I felt afraid, still not sure that I had made the right decision. It was exhausting. How was I going to get through the next few months until I was married, without Tommy here to support me? Thankfully, Tommy called me often from wherever he was ministering, and whenever he asked how I was doing, I would say, "I can make it, Tommy. I know I can make it." I was affirming this truth not just to him, but also to myself; I needed to hear it!

In spite of all my fears, both of Tommy's parents accepted and loved me from the minute they saw me. They were wonderful, especially his mother, Joy. There was an instant bond between us that I couldn't explain. My heart began to soften as the unconditional love that I felt flowing from Joy began to reveal the anger I had unknowingly built up inside over the years against my birth mother. The Lord used her to begin the healing process of my innermost pain and feelings of rejection. It was wonderful to feel so free; I had never felt this way before.

I respected and listened to everything that Joy told me, and I can say, without hesitation, that I couldn't have made it without this wonderful lady. She has been one of the biggest influences in my life. Every morning, she would bring me a tray with coffee, orange juice, toast and vitamins and say "Honey, you're going to need these to be married to my son." She was right. She knew her son, and what he needed in a wife, and did her best to guide me to become the best "ministry" wife that I could be. There are some things in marriage for which no one can prepare you. Thankfully, however, Joy was always there with her words of wisdom and Godly perspective whenever I needed her.

Even with Joy's love and guidance, it was still a very stressful time for me and the adjustment to such a dramatic change in lifestyle didn't come easily at first. I remember having a strong craving to have a cigarette one day. I knew it was totally unacceptable behavior, especially in their house, but I just couldn't help myself. I didn't know how else to cope with the stress that I was feeling, so I locked myself in the bathroom and started to puff away. Joy, who had been looking for me, tried to coax me out for a good fifteen minutes, and in the end, only managed to get me out by reassuring me that if I came out, she wouldn't tell Tommy. Needless to say, that was the last time that I ever touched a cigarette.

She was so cute and understanding about everything. It's like she understood how difficult the transition from my worldly life to the life of ministry was for me. How could she know? She had been raised in a Christian home. Maybe she just knew that the transition to becoming a wife, under any circumstances, is difficult. Perhaps it was that she had seen many like me in their congregation trying to make this change in lifestyle and knew what was ahead. Whatever the reason for her patience and tolerance of me, I was very grateful to have her in my life and I thanked God everyday for her.

The language barrier was a daily challenge for me. Although I had taken English in school, it was completely different talking with Americans in everyday conversation. It took a lot of energy for me to focus on what they were saying, and even more to answer. It really wore me down in those early years, as everything was just so different from what I had been used to; even the simple things seemed hard.

Of course I helped out around the house while I was living with the Barnetts. One day I cleaned the toilet with a "back" brush. Joy saw what I was trying to do and started to try and explain what this brush was used for. Seeing that I was on the verge of tears, not understanding a word she was saying, she just sat on the floor and started laughing. At first I was upset, but then I saw the funny side of what had happened, and I joined her. That's the kind of lady she was: very easy going and always encouraging. We had many moments like this together, when we just had to laugh; she taught me not to take life, or myself, too seriously.

Joy shared with me many years later of how I reminded her of Ruth in the bible, and that she has been blessed by our close mother-daughter relationship, just as Naomi was.

Tommy wanted to take me with him on his next ministry trip overseas and knew that we would have to be married to do so. I agreed to a short engagement and a quick marriage as I didn't want to be away from him either. We thought it would be a great idea to combine our honeymoon with ministry and so it was decided: we would be married as soon as we could make all the arrangements.

Consequently, the weeks leading up to the wedding were like a whirlwind... there was just not enough time to plan things properly. Thankfully, Joy took care of all the fine details for us. We were married on December 12th, 1964, just four months after we had met.

Our wedding day was overwhelming for me. Everything had happened so fast that my parents were not able to make it over in time for the wedding, which really upset me as I wanted my father to meet Tommy and my new family. Most of all, I had hoped he would walk me down the aisle. I was very sad and emotional that they weren't going to be there with me, but I didn't let it overshadow the joy that I felt, and continued on regardless.

There was not time or money to shop for my own wedding gown, so I had to borrow one. It was not at all what I would have chosen for myself. I hated it. I had always seen myself getting married in an elegant Grecian style gown with a long lace veil. Instead, here I was, in a borrowed dress and looking like a marshmallow, even though I only weighed 110 lbs! On top of everything, it was "that time of the month", and I was bloated and cramping so badly that day that I could barely zip the dress up!

On my wedding day I spent five hours at the beauty salon having a permanent. Who does that on the day of her wedding? I thought I'd have plenty of time as we weren't having the ceremony until 8:00p.m. at night. The permanent ended up in a tight afro and it was all I could do to keep it from bouncing out from beneath the veil! To top it all off, my "husband to be," concerned about what the women of the church would think of me, called me at 6:00p.m. to make sure that I wasn't going to wear any makeup! What a ridiculous question! Who doesn't wear makeup everyday, let alone on her wedding day? Rather than getting upset and arguing the point, I decided to take the makeup off and ask him about it later.

Two hours later, I was walking down the aisle on the arm of Tommy's grandfather, cramping, curly, and as white as a sheet. I still remember as I was walking down the aisle asking the Lord, "What am I doing?"

Through Every Season

Tommy's father married us, and I had trouble understanding most of what was being said during the ceremony. Then Tommy, who was nervous and crying, said for "preacher or poorer." I asked him, "Are you sad that you are marrying me?" He said nothing, but just leaned over and kissed me, at which time his dad reminded him sternly, "Son, son we're in church." Everyone laughed, including us.

The rest of the ceremony went on without interruption. Immediately afterwards, I was "kidnapped" by some of the women of the church and driven around the city for hours. I later found out that Tommy had no idea where I was. The ladies said "this is what we do after weddings."

"Really?" I asked.

I was very upset and confused by this new culture and the way they did things, and kept asking "Aren't I supposed to be with my husband?" I was not at all expecting or wanting a tour of the city after just being married, and was so relieved when they finally brought me back to the church. So much for the reception! I was so happy to be back with Tommy again. Everything was going to be okay.

Our wedding night was one I'll always remember...walking around the hotel room all night, trying to relieve the cramping in my stomach to the tune of my new husband's snoring...fantastic!

My New Role as Wife

It got off to a really good start, but got worse as time went on. We fought every day, and every night I would pack my suitcase, then we'd make up, and I'd unpack it again.

The next day we were off to Hawaii for our honeymoon. There had not been time to make any changes to my passport, and consequently we were asked a lot of questions about our relationship to one another by the customs officers, both upon leaving, and returning into the United States. Tommy told them he was a minister and that we were married. We both got some very odd looks of disbelief when they looked at me. I guess even the United States government didn't think that I looked like the wife of a preacher!

Hawaii was the most beautiful place I'd ever seen in my life, and we took many long romantic walks on the beach together. It was just so nice to be alone with him at last. Each morning, I would wake up early before Tommy, brush my teeth, and put on a full face of make up, just so I could look beautiful for him; the things we do when we're first married!

Tommy had planned his next evangelistic crusade months before we met, which would begin in the Philippines, and continue on to Thailand and India.

Tommy was concerned that I might not be ready to go on the mission field with him. His dad reassured him before we left, that after observing me in their home over the past few months, he thought I'd be more than able to cope with the trip overseas. He was right about one thing. I was able to cope with the trip, that wasn't the challenge! After our honeymoon was officially over, we embarked on a three month evangelistic crusade.

It was exciting to be traveling again, and we managed to combine more honeymoon time with Tommy's ministry commitments. Even then, ministry was of utmost importance to him. When he got in front of people to preach, he was totally focused on what he had come to do; to share the message of Jesus Christ with as many as would listen. He was so exciting to watch and I enjoyed going to the meetings with him.

My most vivid memories are of India, where we stayed in a small village in the jungle. There was no hotel for us, just a bungalow which was actually more of a hut with a thatched roof, which we shared with a native boy who cooked for us. There was no bathroom, just a hole in the ground outside. One night, I went outside to go about my business, when a flashlight beamed through the darkness shining right on my bare behind. It was Tommy. What was he thinking? It gave me such a scare that I tinkled all down my leg. I was so annoyed with him. Of course it never crossed my mind that he might be concerned for my safety, as we were in the middle of the jungle, and I realized... *what was I thinking!*

My New Role as Wife

Some of the customs of the Indian people were very odd to me. I remember one time in particular, when we went on a hunting trip, someone killed a huge beast of an animal. As was their custom, they killed it by slitting its throat. I thought it such a horrible thing, having to listen to it groaning as it died a slow death. I wanted my husband to put it out of its misery, but he wouldn't. I was so mad at him. When it finally died, and because there was nowhere else to sit, I had to perch myself on top of the huge animal, in order to pout my displeasure towards them all.

The people of the village were so wonderful. Even though I didn't agree with some of the things that they did, I really loved them. One night they put on a huge feast in our honor. All the little girls were so beautiful. They were fascinated by my blonde hair and red painted finger nails, so I painted all of their nails for them. One of the fourteen year olds did a dance for us in one of my red nightgowns. She was so graceful.

Village life, however, was a strong contrast to city life. Needy people lay starving in the streets. We had seen them as we walked through the city at night. I had never before felt such compassion in my heart. I began to get a glimpse of why my husband was so passionate about reaching hurting people. The same tenacity that had given him the desire to know the Lord at the age of four was now fueling his passion to share the gift of eternal life with the lost. He needed to be sure that he was doing his part to help people find eternal life through Jesus Christ.

It was in India that I realized that this was the life I had said yes to when I married Tommy. A new awareness of who I was, stirred within me. I started to see that it was one thing to know God, but something on a whole other level to serve him. I definitely felt a sense that my life was no longer my own, yet I had no idea how challenging it was going to be for me to rise above my feelings of insecurity, selfishness and inadequacy to meet the call that was on my life. I knew that I was a child of God, but just to make sure, every time Tommy gave an altar call at one of his meetings, I would respond by going forward. He would always tell me "Marja, you don't have to come forward every time I give an altar call, you're saved." He was right, but just like he had felt the need to be reassured as a small child, I also had to make sure.

In the Philippines, we stayed with American missionaries. We started each day at 6:00 a.m. with breakfast, which was way down our list of priorities—we were newlyweds after all!

They made it clear that they were not at all impressed with the way that I dressed. They told Tommy that I looked far too "worldly." Joy had given me some advice on how important it is that women dress modestly and conservatively so as not to draw attention to themselves, but I still couldn't seem to get it right. I was used to dressing to draw attention to myself, and I still wasn't sure what was modest and what wasn't...why wasn't there a manual or something to follow?

Sometimes I felt as if I was made for this new life. Other times however, I felt embarrassed and completely overwhelmed by all the changes and expectations that had been put on me. I decided to take one day at a time. Most of my skirts were too short, but I didn't know how to sew, so I would just let the hem down, unfinished, in an effort to please our hosts. The last thing I wanted to do was be an embarrassment to Tommy.

Even so, my frustrations slowly turned into anger toward Tommy. Why hadn't he told me, *before* he married me, about all the changes I would have to make to live the ministry way of life? I now know that it wasn't fair to blame him, as he probably had never had to be concerned about what women wore until he met me. At the time I felt like nothing I did was right, and hated the way that it made me feel—like a failure.

We fought every day, and every night I would pack my suitcase threatening to go home. Then we'd make up and I'd unpack again. The heavy demand of ministering every night and our constant fighting must have really started to wear Tommy down. Finally one night he said, "Okay then, if you're going to go, just go." I wasn't expecting him to say that! It was then that I made the decision to stay. I'd like to say that I felt the overwhelming presence of God speaking to my heart, telling me that this was where he wanted me to be. The truth of the matter is that I was just plain stubborn! I wasn't about to give up. Looking back, I know that if it hadn't been for the Lord, we would never have made it.

Tommy's schedule included Japan and England, but I started to get very homesick while we were still in the Philippines. He was so good about it, and responded to how I was feeling by taking me to visit my family in Sweden for a week. The first thing that my dad did was offer Tommy a beer, which was his way of welcoming him into his home. My Father wasn't offended when Tommy declined his offer, respecting his position as a man of the cloth. It was difficult for my parents and Tommy to communicate, so I had to interpret everything for them. It was totally frustrating for everyone, and emotionally tiring for me. I kept thinking, *who is going to interpret for me?*

One day, not long after arriving in my hometown, we went into town to look around and ran into some of my old friends. The weather was so cold and we didn't have enough winter clothing with us, so Tommy wore my dad's overcoat, which swamped him as my father was such a big man. I told them that I had married a handsome American, but I'm sure they couldn't understand why, looking at the freezing, red faced young man standing before them. Barely visible inside my dad's huge overcoat, he looked more like a homeless person than the handsome man that I had described. Tommy couldn't wait to leave. He'd had enough of the cold Swedish winter.

Upon returning from our trip, I stayed with Tommy's aunt in Palo Alto, California while he went back to India for more meetings. When he got back, we got into a huge fight over nothing, and this time I packed my bags and left. I flew to San Francisco to stay with my friend Birgitta. We hadn't seen each other since I had left California to be married. I was only there for two days when I realized what a huge mistake I had made. I felt so empty and I couldn't believe how much I missed Tommy. I called him crying and asked him to please forgive me and take me back. He said yes. Thank God for forgiveness!

This was the turning point in our marriage. Despite all our differences, we both felt such a strong sense of purpose for our marriage as we reflected on all that the Lord had done to bring us together. Right then, we made the decision that we were going to stay together, no matter what. We had no idea how greatly God was going to use us, and how significant this unified decision, so early in our marriage, was in setting the pace for our future. We prayed a simple prayer together, asking the Lord to help us with our marriage. We meant every word, and knew that the Lord had heard us and would bless us.

Tommy's father had invited him to come to Kansas City to help him with his church, as the assistant pastor, instead of continuing with the ministry that Tommy had built for himself as an evangelist. Tommy agreed that this would be a good idea; there was so much he could learn from his dad. So off we went to Kansas City.

We had our own house, a big house, but with not much furniture. All we had was what people from the church had given us. Tommy spent a lot of time at the church helping his dad, who gave him a small salary. When he wasn't there he worked at a gas station and chopped trees to help support us, and did whatever it took to provide for me physically, financially and spiritually.

It was quite an experience getting into the day to day routine of married life in a new home and new city. I had never learned to cook, so for the first three months we had Swedish pancakes every day, for every meal. I tried to make them interesting by using different fruits and flavors, and was true to my name, which means "a berry." I blended in every type of berry that I could find to add some variety to those pancakes!! Even so, they were still just pancakes! Tommy was very patient with me, but I'm sure he must have been wondering how long this would last. It's hilarious looking back, but at the time it was not at all funny, especially for my poor Tommy.

Only later, in hindsight, could I really appreciate how difficult being married to me was for him, especially after getting to know his mom who was the perfect wife in all areas; he was probably expecting me to be like her!

I recall one instance when I finally decided to try one of Joy's recipes for a good home cooked meal; round steak and mashed potatoes, instead of pancakes. My husband was really looking forward to coming home that night to taste what I had prepared. I felt so bad when he tried to cut into the steak only to find that it was as hard as leather. He shouted "you could kill a person with it, it's so hard!" At first I thought he was joking, but he wasn't! He was so tired and hungry... and now he was really angry. I had tried my best and failed. I burst into tears and ran to our room. Joy, who had been there helping, came after me and simply said "Marja, it's going to be ok, I understand." Although I felt comforted, my husband stayed angry with me the whole night!

I kept trying to cook and slowly, I got better. Today I'm a great cook and love to prepare his favorite dishes for him whenever he's at home.

The women of the church received me very well, but I didn't make any close friends. My mother-in-law, Joy, became my closest friend. She nurtured me and continued to teach me practical things like how to cook and be a good wife for my husband. Tommy continued to travel as an evangelist around the United States on and off for the next three years.

It was a very lonely time for me and I was still very insecure, but I kept on trusting that God knew what he was doing in my life. I spent a lot of time reading the word and praying. I got better at my English and the more time I spent with God, the more my relationship with him, and Tommy, began to flourish. It was in this lonely time that I learned what a true and faithful friend I had in the Lord, and that he was and always would be with me when I needed him.

In 1965, my adoptive parents came to America to visit me. They were keen to meet Tommy, so we both met them in New York and then traveled together back through Texas and then on to Kansas City to meet Tommy's parents. Once again, I was the interpreter, but didn't mind at all. Everyone got along so well. I really enjoyed having them here with me. It was sad to see them leave, and after they left, it took me a while to settle back into my routine again.

There were still a lot of changes that were really hard for me to deal with, many of which I only found out about once we were married. One was the "no makeup or jewelry" in church rule. This may seem like it shouldn't have been such a big deal, but coming from a country like Sweden, where all the girls wore high heels and makeup, I was just not ready for the complete transition to chewing gum and wearing sneakers!

When I was twenty-six years old, I took a job modeling in a high end fashion store in Kansas City. My job was to walk around in designer clothing, like Christian Dior, modeling the latest fashions available in the store. One day, I was asked if I would like to do some photographic modeling. I hadn't done any photographic work for years, and I thought this would be a great opportunity to get back into it. Tommy didn't mind me working part time, as long as I was there for him when he got home from work, he was happy. It felt wonderful to be out of the house and the extra money helped us make ends meet.

However, the way I looked as a model in the stores

was a strong contrast to the way I was expected to present myself to our congregation on Sundays.

Before every service, Tommy would literally inspect me to make sure I wasn't wearing any make up or jewelry. I would always comply at home, but once we got to the meeting, I would go into the restroom or the back of the church and put my makeup on and then take it off before I saw him again. I didn't see this as rebellion. I just couldn't understand why it was such a big deal for him, or the church. I understood the reasoning behind not trying to attract attention to ourselves by wearing make up, but couldn't quite see how walking around pale and ugly achieved that objective either! There had to be a happy medium somewhere? At the time I didn't realize how important it was to Tommy for me to be the model ministry wife. The way he had been raised taught him that makeup and jewelry were just not necessary to show a woman's beauty.

I remember one time getting ready to attend a General Council meeting with his parents, not long after returning from our honeymoon. I was excited to be able to dress up and wore a tight fitting suit and high heels. Tommy was so upset by the way that I looked and refused to let me go down to the meeting if I was going to be dressed "like that." We had a big fight and he told his mother that I was going to ruin him by the way I dressed. My mother-in-law, who was always so supportive of me, simply said, "She looks good." He ended up going down to the meeting alone with his dad, while Joy stayed with me in the room.

It was ironic to me that the very look that had attracted him to me in the beginning, now seemed to be causing him so much inner conflict. Now looking back, I can see that Tommy put a lot of pressure on himself to impress his peers, which overflowed into our marriage and his expectations of me as his wife. A long time later, he told me that he was afraid that I was too stylish and classy for the other pastors' wives and he didn't want to make them feel bad. I learned then that he cared deeply about how other people felt, and not so much about what they thought, as I had assumed.

Once I understood where he was coming from, I made an extra special effort to dress so that he would be proud of me. I learned how to dress appropriately, yet still keep my own personal style; we could both be happy. This new lifestyle wasn't that bad after all, it was just very different to the way I had been used to living. It would take a bit of adjusting on my part, but I knew I could do it; Tommy and I could make it together!

The Beginning of a Legacy

Even though we had agreed to make our marriage work no matter what, the early years were still tough, and I wanted to leave so many times. Whenever I would start to feel like I couldn't make it, I would remind myself that where I was right now, was where I was supposed to be. It was not important for me to know what the entire plan for my life was. Tommy was the beginning of the answer to my prayer before coming to America and it was now clear that we were to be together: this was the Lord's plan for me. I have told Tommy many times over the years, that if I hadn't married him, I believe I would probably have ended up just like my mother, who married five times after my father.

Looking back, I think that what I experienced in the first few years of our marriage was a huge feeling of loss. What I went through was a grieving process at the loss of the lifestyle that I loved, and also the dreams that I had for myself. Finally, working through this process led me to a place of acceptance of my new life. It took patience from Tommy and a lot of time spent with the

Lord in prayer, but finally things started to settle down and I felt I was ready to become a mother.

During a revival meeting in St Louis, in the fall of 1967, I rushed off to the bathroom feeling sick. When I got back to my seat I whispered to Tommy that I thought I was pregnant. He was so excited that he announced it to the whole meeting with a huge smile on his face; I hadn't even been to the doctor yet! Happily the doctor confirmed that I was right; I was going to be a mom. My pregnancy was very easy, with not one stretch mark or a single craving that I can remember. I did, however, gain a lot of weight, which was hard to accept as I had always had a trim figure. I tried not to think too much about the weight that I didn't seem to have any control of, or the actual birth, and kept myself as busy and active as I could.

One night, we were playing board games at Tommy's parents' house, when I started to go into labor at around 10:00 p.m. We called the doctor when my contractions were about ten minutes apart, but he told us to wait until they were a little closer. I'd never felt anything like this before, no one had warned me about how painful it would be! Finally when they were at five minute intervals, the doctor said it was time to make our way to the hospital. My suitcase had been packed since the baby's due date two weeks earlier and we were ready to go, but were both really nervous now that it was time to finally meet our baby.

The ride to the hospital was hilarious... I was so afraid that if I sat down I would crush the baby's head, so I squatted all the way, not sitting once. Halfway to the hospital we got a flat tire and the police had to come and escort us the rest of the way. It was like something out of a movie! Eventually, we got to the hospital. Needless to say, I was just thankful that I hadn't delivered the baby in the car.

In those days, husbands weren't allowed in the labor room, so I suffered alone for seven hours. Our daughter was born on June 25, 1968, and it was the best thing that I had ever experienced; she was just so beautiful! When Tommy came to my room after seeing the baby through the glass of the nursery, he said proudly "She smiled at me and wiggled her head." Since then she has never stopped smiling; what a joy she is! When it came to naming her, we decided that Tommy should choose her first name as I didn't know many American names, and I then would choose her middle name, so together we named her Kristie Kaarina Barnett.

Being a mother for the first time was exciting and tiring all at once. To my amazement, the very next day, Tommy went to play in a golf tournament. I was so angry with him, how could he leave me alone so soon after giving birth to our first child? Kristie suffered from colic for the first few months, and would not stop crying. On top of this, she had her days and nights mixed up and never wanted to sleep when I did! Of course I had no idea that babies didn't necessarily fit into our schedules; this was a whole new learning curve, not just for me, but for Tommy, also.

Kristie absolutely hated to be in restaurants, and would not stop crying until we left. Often, when we were out with Tommy's parents, Joy would take her outside to calm her down so that we could finish our meals in peace. Despite the constant crying, she was a wonderful baby, and once her colic settled down, I began to really enjoy being a mom. She was cute when she would say "ut" instead of "up" and "I want to say some more" instead of "I want some more." Maybe some of my broken English had something to do with it!

From day one, it felt right to speak only English to Kristie. I'm not sure why, but I never felt the need to speak to her in my own native language. In our home, I only reverted back to speaking Swedish when I was mad, but would quickly change back to English once I realized that no one had a clue what all the screaming was about! To this day, my kids love to mimic and make fun of me.

My first opportunity to go back to Sweden since becoming "Mrs Tommy Barnett," came in 1969, as Tommy was going to be away on a mission trip to India for a few months. As I was not too far along in my pregnancy to restrict my ability to travel, the timing seemed perfect. I'd kept in touch with my family during the years that I had been away, but even so, I always longed for the time when I would be able to go home to visit them, especially now that I had started a family of my own.

The plane ride to Sweden was very long and challenging as Kristie was still a baby and I was pregnant with our second child. The air pressure in the cabin hurt Kristie's ears and I couldn't get her to settle no matter what I tried. A lady sitting behind me came forward and said, "bless your heart, let me help you." She looked very familiar; then I realized who she was. It was Rose Marie, who played Sally Rogers, one of the comic writers on the Dick Van Dyke show. She was so sweet, taking Kristie gently in her arms, giving me a welcome break.

The years had been eventful and busy for me and there was so much to share about my new life in America. Things in Sweden, however, seemed to move at a much slower pace than I remembered. It was great to see my family and friends again, but they all seemed to be doing the same things they were when I left five years ago. The life that I had once thought was so exciting was now dull in comparison to my life in America with Tommy. I had finally satisfied my need to answer the question that I had asked myself so many times over and over; "did I make the right choice?" It was this trip that confirmed that I had, and I couldn't wait to get home to Tommy. I returned to America with a peaceful resolve that I hadn't had before. I wouldn't trade my new life or country for anything.

We were going to wait awhile before having another child, but God had a different plan! Thirteen months after Kristie was born, on July 14, 1969, our first son arrived right on time, after only four hours of labor. Tommy named the 8lbs 10oz bundle of joy, Luke Whig, after his dad's middle name. At school, years later, Luke would get embarrassed about his middle name, and to avoid having to say it, he would introduce himself as "Luke W. Barnett," which I always thought made him sound so grown up and important.

Kristie was beautiful, but when I saw Luke, I thought he had to be the most gorgeous baby that I had ever seen. He just had a look about him that was so special. Not even photographs that I have of him as a baby do justice to what a sweet, beautiful face and ready smile he had. As if to confirm that it was not just a case of a mother's biased opinion, he was named the "prettiest boy" in Kansas City in a baby competition when he was only twelve months old.

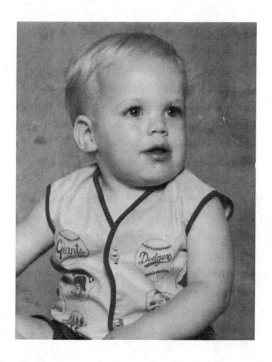

Of course Tommy adored Kristie, but he was so proud to finally have a son to carry on the Barnett name. Kristie, however, was not at all impressed with Luke. She liked being the only child and was jealous of this intruder who was taking the attention away from her. She was a typical first child and took a long time to accept him.

Luke always seemed to be getting into mischief. At two years old he jumped off the sofa straight onto a glass top coffee table. There was blood everywhere and we had to rush him to hospital to get stitches. Then at the age of four, the Lord used Luke to test my faith... and Tommy's.

Luke had been in the garage playing. He came running in to me coughing with something running down the sides of his mouth. He said "Mommy, I drank some gas!" which I later discovered had in fact been antifreeze. I didn't know what to do, but remembered, *"They will pick up snakes with their hands; and when they drink deadly poison, it will not hurt them at all; they will place their hands on sick people and they will get well."* (Mark 16:18, NIV) That said it all, so I lay my hands on Luke and prayed that the Lord would heal him.

As far as I was concerned, it was done. So I sent him off to play and got on with my day. When Tommy got home, I told him what had happened. He panicked and got so angry with me. We rushed straight to the hospital, where the doctors were also angry with me. I couldn't understand why everyone was so upset, as Luke was fine. The hospital continued to do tests on him for a full week. All of the results of the tests showed that he had not been harmed in any way. It cost my husband $400: an expensive lesson in faith. We always joke that Luke will never have a problem when it comes to cold weather; he will never freeze!

In 1971, Tommy accepted the position of Pastor to the Westside Assembly of God church in Davenport, Iowa. Tommy felt that it was time to build his own church based on the soul winning principles that he had seen exemplified in his father's church in Kansas City. Tommy went on ahead of me as I was sick, and I joined him two days later.

Upon arrival, I took one look at the church and asked, "Tommy, are you sure about this?" It was small with peeling paint and broken windows and only had seventy-six members. There was a lot of work to be done to build the congregation and get the building in order. Still, I trusted Tommy's decision to move there, and if anyone could rebuild a church, I believed my husband could. He had so much energy and poured himself into making the Westside Assembly of God the best church that he could.

Dressing appropriately for church was still a challenge. I tried so hard to get everything right for my first Sunday, wearing a plain white dress with long sleeves, my hair up in a knot, light lipstick and the tiniest amount of mascara. Tommy took one look at me and chuckled, "You still look worldly. What am I going to do with you?" No matter what I wore, I looked different to everyone else, especially in the mid-west! In the end, I stopped trying to please everyone and dressed to suit myself, just a little more toned down.

I wondered what the people of the church would be like, and was not looking forward to having to meet new people once again. Tommy encouraged me to make a greater effort to be more warm, open and compassionate, recognizing that in my Swedish culture, people were not as "huggy" as they are in America. I made a conscious effort to be more open and relaxed with people and found that even though it was still difficult to communicate verbally, a smile and a friendly hug went a long way to bridging the gap.

As Tommy shared his vision with the church, people with the same heart began to rise up from within the congregation in response to the call to "win souls". It was amazing to watch and I was very proud to be his wife and be part of what he was doing.

Tommy believed that everything he needed to make the ministry successful and grow was within the church, or the "Miracle in the House" principle as he now calls it. He has always exuded energy, creativity and passion and with his three associate Pastors, Harold Heffelfinger, Bill Wilson and Doug Duncan by his side, they were a formidable force for the Kingdom of God. Together they would think of creative ways to draw people into the church, and sometimes I wondered where it would all stop.

One time the church made a one hundred yard banana split for the children to eat as part of a promotional Sunday, which actually made the *Guinness Book of World Records*! Another time they constructed a popcorn ball as big as a boulder. As if that wasn't novel enough, another time they made a bigger than life, giant popsicle. I'm not sure that any of these were exactly sanitary, but they certainly did the job of drawing people to the church so that Tommy could share the gospel of Jesus Christ with them!

Over the years, there were countless ways that Tommy and his team came up with to attract people to come and check out Westside, and ultimately, what God was all about.

They staged tugs-of-war, squirt gun fights, pilgrimages to the zoo. They enticed young people to come and try to win a mini bike, trips to amusement parks and to compete for prizes in arm-wrestling and skateboarding.

Winning souls for Jesus is the driving force that underlines Tommy's reason for doing anything, and if it isn't going to be effective to win souls, he doesn't do it. He decided early on in ministry that he wasn't going to have a church full of Christians to preach to every week. The church's philosophy was to use anything to reach people as long as it was in good taste and it glorified God.

Of course there were people who criticized the church for it's reliance on gimmicks to attract the crowds, but they never deterred Tommy. He believes with all his heart that using so called "gimmicks" attracts people who might not otherwise come to church, and faced with the alternative of saying, "we're having church tonight, please come?" I know which one he'd choose every time! His favorite saying is "the method is not sacred, just the message."

As the church grew, Tommy and his team responded by constructing buildings to house all the people and activities that were being created: four building projects in total.

In those early days he did everything from preaching to running the Sunday school classes for the kids. Tommy would happily go off to work each morning, devoting all of his time and energy to the development and building of the new church. He was a very hard worker and the days were long. He always came home to have dinner with us and spend time with the kids before they went to bed and then return to church, sometimes not getting home until well after 10:00 p.m. After a day of "baby talk" with the kids, I really looked forward to him walking through the door, but I learned to let him unwind for at least half an hour before I started talking to him. I would always make sure that I looked and smelled nice for him; I wanted him to always look forward to coming home to me.

Tommy had told me early in our marriage that he needed me to be a mother and support to him by keeping our home "together." He said that he didn't need me to play the piano, or join the choir like so many other pastors' wives did. My ministry was to be the best wife and mom that I could be. This turned out to be a perfect fit for me, as I always felt fulfilled as a mom and loved being with my kids. Being there for them and my husband whenever they needed me became the most important thing in my life. It was the role that the Lord was asking of me... and it was just for a season—or so I thought.

I enjoyed helping with the make up and costumes for the special pageants at Christmastime and Easter. Tommy's sister, Vicki, who is six years younger than Tommy, would often help me out with gowns from her exclusive bridal shop. It was always great to spend time with her. I also spoke at the local "Woman Aglow" meetings a couple of times, but other than that, I preferred to be at home to look after my family. These were very lonely years for me as we lived quite a long way out of town. Once again, as it had also been in Kansas City, the Lord used this alone time to draw me closer to him. I spent a lot of time during the day, in between chores and kids, reading the Bible and praying.

I didn't drive until I was thirty-two years old. I learned to drive at a local driving school in our town and passed the theory test of one hundred questions the very first time I took it. My kids still make fun of me because I drive with both feet, the left for the brake and the right for the accelerator, that's just the way they taught me. My first car was a purple Opal, it was the ugliest car in the world, but I was so grateful to finally be able to venture out of the house when I felt like it instead of having to rely on someone else. I loved being independent.

I did have a few mishaps though. I was stopped for speeding a couple of times by a police officer, who coincidentally attended our church. The first time, I told him that I had just bought ice cream and was afraid that if I didn't get it home, it would melt! Another time, I cited having to keep up with my husband, Tommy Barnett, as the reason why I was going so fast! He let me off both times, and even though these were valid, truthful reasons, I'm not sure I would have gotten away with it had I not been Tommy's wife.

Dale Lane and his wife Lynn first attended our church with their two young daughters, Lisa and Michelle, in 1973. Dale had worked as a bus director at a satellite bus ministry to our church and had a heart for soul winning.

After spending time with Tommy, they all felt a ministry kinship, sharing a vision to win the lost to Christ and reach hurting people. It wasn't long before they decided to make the move to Westside from the soul winning, outreach focused, Baptist church which they currently attended. Lynn became Tommy's secretary and they quickly became our close friends. We were united by a common vision greater than ourselves: to win souls for Jesus.

Jo Lummer also became my close friend and mentor during these early years as a Pastor's wife. We met at a luncheon after her husband Paul's father's funeral. Tommy and Paul's brother had been friends for many years. After chatting for a while, Jo and I found out that we both went to the same spa, so we started going there together. She worked alongside Lynn, as Tommy's secretary, helping to keep him organized. Many times when I was upset, I would call her and she would help me to get a better perspective on what I was struggling with. We always knew that we could count on each other.

I remember on one occasion especially, when I was very upset, calling Jo while she was at work at the church office. She came immediately, no questions asked, telling Tommy that I needed her and she'd be back as soon as possible. Jo took me to a place that she often went to when she needed time to think: the "Figge Art Gallery." It had a nice room upstairs that overlooked a park. It was a very serene, quiet place. Unbeknownst to Jo, we walked into the gallery and were shocked to see that the current exhibition was a display of black and white photos of nude people! Both of our mouths dropped open and we started laughing (which is not appropriate in an art gallery). Of course we weren't laughing at the art, but at the fact that the pastor's wife from the largest Assembly of God church in the country and his secretary were there.

We made our way upstairs, where we continued to laugh. You know, I don't think the problem was ever talked about... there was no need to. You see, sometimes laughter with a good friend brings relief to a troubled soul. I don't think either one of us will ever forget that day in the Figge Art Gallery in Davenport, Iowa. That's what I love about Jo. She never responded in a churchy way, but always with encouragement, sensitivity and love, often reaffirming, "you are a strong woman, you can get through this time."

One time, Wayne Newton was in Davenport and we thought it would be fun to go to his concert. The son of a couple in our church was his promoter and managed to get us great seats; front row, center.

We were all big fans of his and were excited to be seeing him in person. After a few songs, he started to make his way down from the stage and came towards us. Perhaps it was the huge red flower that I had in my hair that was attracting him to us, but whatever the reason, when he reached for my hand, I felt myself begin to rise up from my chair. At the same time, I could feel someone holding on to the hem of my skirt, stopping me from moving anywhere. It was Jo, my protector, probably scared that my photo swooning over this pop idol would make the front page of the local newspapers!

Jo and I ran a charm class for the young ladies in our church. With all the people coming to church on our buses from the streets, we saw a need to help the girls learn how to dress in an appropriate way for church. Who better to teach them than me? After all, I completely understood the challenges they were facing from my own personal experiences. We used the book The Christian Charm Course as our guide, which, amongst other things, encouraged the practice of walking with a book on your head for good posture. I would often buy items of clothing for the girls to wear to get them started. It was fun, and it felt good to be able to help others in a way that I felt only I could.

At this time, my clothing allowance from Tommy was just $10.00 a month. At a time when a pair of shoes cost $5.91 and a dress was $6.99, it didn't stretch very far at all. I became a great Salvation Army shopper and always managed to find a bargain.

One thing I wasn't good at was disciplining my children. In Sweden it was against the law to spank a child, so spanking was a foreign concept to me. Instead I would try to be firm with my words, using the voice of reason to explain to them what was right and wrong. However, it was a different story once their dad got home. Tommy's dad had been very strict with him as a child, so he had no trouble being the one to enforce the discipline in our family. The kids knew that once their father got home, they would get a spanking, and it wouldn't be soft! He was a great deterrent and it worked really well for our family. I never had to deal with the spankings, which suited me fine. I really didn't have it in me!

Our third child, Matthew West (after the Westside church) was born on January 22nd, 1974. In my eighth month, the doctors told me that they were having trouble hearing a regular heartbeat. At this news, the entire church started to pray, and two weeks later when I was tested again, he had regained a strong, healthy heartbeat. The doctor continued to keep me under observation, and when he was finally born he had to stay in the hospital for a whole week as he was so yellow with jaundice. They covered his eyes and tied up his hands and told me that he could be retarded or even die as it was such a severe case.

I had been told after Luke was born that with my particular blood type, there was an increased risk for the babies to be more severely affected by jaundice with each pregnancy. After all the trouble that I had with Matthew's birth, the doctors advised me not to have any more children and Tommy and I both agreed. My tubes were tied right after Matthew was born and our family was complete.

It was heartbreaking to have to leave him at the hospital, and I visited him every day. He was the only one of my children whose name I chose. I named him Matthew, gift from God, because he had nearly died, but the Lord gave him back to me.

Matthew developed a lazy eye and I didn't realize that the kids at school had been teasing him about it until one day he came home and said softly, "Mommy, I'm not

Chinese am I?" He was so cute, and even though I had a little chuckle inside, looking into his slightly crooked blue eyes, I could see that what they had said had really affected him. He was so young and I couldn't stand that he was hurting. I wanted so badly to go to the school and defend my baby, but of course I didn't! I just prayed with him and asked the Lord to help him to stand up for himself against all adversity. Unknowingly, I was praying a blessing over my son that would be needed in an even greater capacity many years later when he became the Pastor of the Los Angeles International Dream Center.

One day, on our way to register Matthew for Little League, he leaned forward and asked," Hey! How come we've been having my birthday on the wrong month?" He had been studying his birth certificate in the back seat of the car and read that he was born in January and not February as we all believed. I immediately responded, "Don't be silly, I should know when you were born; I'm your mother." But sure enough, there it was in black and white, January 22nd. We all laughed hysterically. I couldn't believe that I'd made such a huge mistake. The poor boy was already thinking that he was Chinese and now his family didn't even know which month he was born! He couldn't believe that his own mother couldn't remember what month she had given birth to him! The family joke after that was that Matthew was adopted and we had many laughs over that incident. We'd been celebrating his birthday on the wrong month for seven years, what a family!

Top left: On bike
Top right: Little Marja
Bottom: With adoptive parents

Top: Wedding day
Bottom left: Adoptive parents visit U.S.A.
Bottom right: Luke & Kristie

Top left: Tommy and I
Top right: Tommy and I
Bottom: Tommy and I on TBN

Top: On the run to LA
Middle: Prayer pavillion
Bottom: Marge Atkins

Top: Me goofing around
Bottom left: Judy Rhodes
Bottom right: JoAnn Denman

Top: Dori Grantham
Middle: Sharon Henning
(behind Tommy)
Bottom: Nancy Hinkle

Top left: Lynn Lane
Top right: Faithe Tines
Bottom: Jo Lummer

Top left: Donna Unicume
Top right: With Kristie and Kent Jr.
Bottom: With Kristie and Joy

Top: Chase, Chantelle, & Kent Jr.
Bottom left: Tommy and Kristie
Bottom right: Aubrey

Top left: AnnaLee
Top right: Caden & Mia
Bottom left: Family
Bottom right: Family

Top: Family
Bottom left: Tommy and I
Bottom right: Tommy and I

Top: Tommy and I
Bottom middle: Tommy and I
Bottom: Tommy and I

Top: Tommy and Kent Jr.
Middle: Tommy and I
Bottom: Tommy and I

Top: Tommy, my pastor
Bottom left: Marja
Bottom right: Marja

Top: Marja
Bottom left: Marja
Bottom right: Marja

Top left: Marja
Top right: With Matthew in NY
Bottom: Luke and Tommy

Stand and Be Counted

We had stood on the word of God and he had seen us through. "Submit yourselves, then, to God. Resist the devil, and he will flee from you." (James 4:7, NIV)

In 1977, when the kids were eight, seven and two yrs old, our family experienced one of the most challenging, faith-building years of our lives.

It all started one day when my husband took one of the boys to get a haircut. In the barber shop our son picked up a magazine, which Tommy quickly realized was hardcore pornography. Shortly after this incident, he made a trip to the store to pick up some flour and noticed a whole row in the magazine section designated to pornography.

He came home and was infuriated about how this trashy material was being displayed right out in the open. Families should be able to bring children to the barber shop or grocery store without the fear of having to protect their children and themselves from what they see. I agreed with him on this point, but we were not in agreement, for the first time in our marriage, on what he was proposing to do next.

That week, at the Sunday night service, he preached a message called "We Want Our Rights" and spoke of how in this day and age everyone wants their rights; women, minorities, homosexuals. You name it, they want rights! He explained that as the Body of Christ, we should have the right to be able to go to stores without having to worry about being confronted with illicit print media.

He followed his sermon with a plan for the congregation to boycott the stores where they shopped, unless the stores agreed to remove all the pornographic material or relocate it out of sight within the next few weeks. Tommy wanted our people to do it in a gracious, courteous manner, but with firmness. The members were to inform the shop owners that their Pastor would be keeping a list of the stores that comply, and the list would be posted at the back of our church to encourage the patronage of these stores.

The next day it was all over the newspapers, "Barnett Declares War on Pornography."

And that's exactly what happened. Our congregation rose to the challenge and did exactly as Tommy had asked. Within weeks, the five major grocery chains had all complied with our church's wishes. Other churches joined us, crossing denominational barriers for the common cause of cleaning up our stores in Davenport for Christ.

It didn't stop there, however. My husband has such a gift of being able to encourage and inspire people and the young people really started to get fired up. They asked my husband for permission to go witnessing into the areas where the massage parlors and adult bookstores were.

Tommy went to the County Attorney to check if it was legal for the kids to do what they were proposing to do, and got the green light. The kids stood outside the parlors and adult bookstores, handing out tracts to people on their way in to the stores, often convicting them. In many cases people passed by the stores completely.

Our church and its people were really making an impact on the community. A couple of times things got a bit rough, but with great results in the end. One of our young men was handing out tracts outside one of the adult stores and said to one patron, "Jesus loves you," and with that, the man struck him across the mouth, knocking him to the ground. The young man just stood back up and said "Mister, Jesus still loves you." The man went home, but couldn't sleep and kept hearing the words of the young man saying "Jesus loves you." The following Wednesday night, the man came to our church prayer meeting and came to the front and testified of what had happened the week before. His life was turned around for the Lord because of the boldness of one young man, not afraid to stand for what he believed.

The young people continued on with their campaign. On one occasion, they were confronted by the local police and told that if they didn't get off the streets, they would be put in jail. They called to ask my husband what they should do, and he said "Carry on, what you are doing is legal." The next call my husband received was to say that all nine of our young people had been arrested, and were in jail.

Tommy rushed down to the jail and confronted the officer in charge, stating that he was the one in trouble as we had received permission from the county attorney for our young people to be on the streets. No sooner had he said this than the officer received a call to say that where the others had been, there were now thirty-six more in their place. My husband continued to say that if the officer did not release them by tomorrow night, there would be thirteen hundred moms and dads joining the thirty-six.

The officer responded "If you get them all off the streets right now, I will help you get an ordinance against the bookstores and massage parlors developed." Tommy agreed. Once again, the church made the newspaper headlines with "Police arrest the Westside nine." Within three weeks the city passed an ordinance that literally shut those places down. All the press wrote favorable reports about us. One paper said "It is time that instead of throwing kids in jail, they should reward them with a medal for doing what the city fathers did not have the courage to do."

Just when it seemed like we had had a complete victory, things started to get really ugly. The massage parlors were owned by some very undesirable underworld crime figures. We started to get letters and phone calls threatening to blow up our church and shoot my husband in the pulpit. I was very afraid for Tommy and my children. Everything that I had feared would happen was becoming a reality. Next, threats came that they were going to kill our children! I was horrified and angry with Tommy for putting our family at risk. "How could this be worth the price that we were now paying personally," I asked? We moved our children to a country school hoping that they would be safe out of the city. The threats continued to come. We received a disgusting letter with filthy pictures depicting what they would do to me while Tommy was out of town if he didn't stop his campaign against the massage parlors and adult bookstores.

I could not believe what was happening to us; it was like something out of a movie! Before each meeting, the police would sweep the church for bombs of all things, and during the service there would be agents in the balcony! I have never been more afraid in my life. At night a helicopter would fly over our house as a precaution and we had wire across our doorways to alert us if anyone intruded into our home. In the middle of it all, Tommy had to go to Pennsylvania to preach.

Across the road from where we lived was a new development with a lot of construction work in progress. One day, one of the workers came to warn me saying that he had noticed someone watching me with binoculars, and then follow me when I left the house. A few days later, on my way home from shopping, a man chased me in my car forcing me to the side of the road. I had only recently received my driver's license and was still not very confident behind the wheel. I definitely hadn't been trained to deal with high speed road chases! I jumped out of the car and ran until I came to a farmhouse. I rushed through the door with the man in hot pursuit behind me. Once inside, I explained to the startled woman that I was being chased and needed help. She just looked at me stunned. She explained that only minutes before, she had locked and chained the door *and* bolted it shut;

there was no way that I could have just "come in." And yet I had, and without any effort! It was a miracle. The Lord had gone before me and made the way straight! We both stared at each other in amazement for a minute and then I called Tommy. Thank God I didn't have any of the children with me, I hate to think what could have happened if I did.

When Tommy got back from his trip, he was furious. After tracking the offender down using the car license plate number that the construction worker had given to us, he went straight to the man's house. Tommy spoke to him face to face, telling him that if I got a cold, or any of the kids got sick, or if anyone hurt his family, he would not be responsible for what would happen to him. We didn't have any more problems of this kind after Tommy's warning.

On top of all this, the massage parlors sent a lawyer to sue us for trying to shut them down, but the Lord had a different plan for him. Ironically, he was saved in our church and became our church attorney! It seemed that everything that the enemy did to try and hurt us was turned for our good and for the Lord's glory. "And we know that in all things God works for the good of those who love him, who have been called according to His purpose" (Romans 8:28, NIV). We made headlines, and the national news, all telling of what was happening through our church in Davenport, Iowa. Christians united with us in support with prayer and public opinion was on our side. It was a very scary time, but the Lord had seen us all through safely. Today the ordinance still stands.

We had stood on the word of God and He had seen

us through. "Submit yourselves, then, to God. Resist the devil, and he will flee from you" (James 4:7, NIV). Even though we had not been in agreement going into this battle, I was very proud of Tommy for the way that he had stood with such conviction against evil. He and I became closer than we had ever been before and I had a new respect for him as my husband and my Pastor. The Lord used the events of the past few months to increase our faith in him. We now knew him as our protector and defender. In the end, it was a well publicized, awesome testimony to the Glory of God.

There were many happy times spent with our congregation during our time in Davenport. One time in particular stands out as a milestone in our ministry together.

It was 1976, and we were about to experience the manifestation of what the Lord tells us in his word, "But I, when I am lifted up from the earth, will draw all men to myself" (John 12:32, NIV).

A few years earlier, at a time when his life was torn by drugs and alcohol, country music singer Johnny Cash, attended a meeting in Tennessee where Tommy was preaching. A few weeks later he returned to that church and stayed behind afterward and sought Tommy out and they began to form a friendship. He came back a couple of weeks later after Tommy's next revival, and accepted the Lord as his personal savior. Shortly after that, Johnny came to Davenport on a singing tour, and Tommy asked if he'd come to sing at a giant Sunday school rally that we were planning to hold at the John O'Donnell Stadium. He agreed. He gave a testimony on the role the church had played in his life and with his group the Tennessee Three and the Carter family, they sang an assortment of gospel songs and Cash hits.

With the thought "the method is not sacred, just the message" foremost in his mind, Tommy then stepped forward, wasting no time capitalizing on the huge crowd of well over twenty thousand people that had gathered to hear this popular man of the day sing. He preached a message declaring, "God has been good to you. He loves you... if you'll just turn your life to Jesus Christ, He will save you." When Tommy gave the altar call, close to five thousand people responded, coming forward out of their seats to the sound of Johnny Cash and the Tennessee Three singing "come home, come home," from the gospel song "Supper Time."

It was an incredible sight, one I will never forget, and will go down in history as one of the largest single crowds at any event in Davenport ever. He gave Tommy a bronzed spike (nail) with his name on it, which he still treasures to this day. It was a very exciting time for all involved, and was the talking point of the area for many years to come.

All of Tommy's hard work and creativity had paid off, as the Westside Assembly of God had become one of the fastest growing churches in America, multiplying to over four thousand people in just seven years. We had no idea that the Lord was about to move us to another level in ministry; how could it get any better than this?

It was at this high point in our ministry when Tommy received an invitation to Pastor the Phoenix

First Assembly of God church in Arizona. He had been to Phoenix to speak one time before, in the middle of the summer, and had decided that he never wanted to go to Phoenix again, as the heat was stifling.

Soon after receiving the invitation, Tommy met with Jo to get her advice, valuing her input, as her father had pastored Phoenix First Assembly years before. He had almost completely discarded the idea of taking the position, evidenced by the crumpled letter that he retrieved from the trash can to show her. She read it, and he asked her for her thoughts. Jo's first response was that the church in Davenport would be devastated if he left, but on the other hand, it was an awesome opportunity. He had already rebuilt Westside, exceeding all expectations, and she saw no reason why he couldn't do the same with the flagging Phoenix First Assembly. It could be great again; if anyone could breathe life back into it, Tommy could. Tommy immediately asked Jo to talk with Paul about making the move with us and for her to continue as his secretary. They both agreed to come with us, and we were elated.

Before leaving Davenport, Tommy was given the key to the city and received the Man of the Year award for his service and contribution to the community. It was a fitting end to a season that had evoked so much personal growth in both of us, and the congregation of people that we had grown to love, and were now leaving behind.

This Time, This Place, This People

Tommy made the first trip to Phoenix for his interview by himself. He then brought me over to see what I thought; my first impression was that it was the hottest place that I'd ever been.

We had made the decision to make the move to Phoenix together. It wasn't an easy decision for Tommy to make, as the church in Davenport was thriving and he loved the people. He had been through so much with them, and they loved him just as much as he did them. It didn't really make sense to leave the congregation of four thousand and move to a church with only two hundred fifty people, and which had had four to five church splits in as many years, but he loved a challenge.

The deciding factor for Tommy was the word he received from the Lord in his prayer time saying, "I want you to leave your child. I will give you, as I did Abraham, one hundredfold of what I gave you in Davenport, Iowa." He was sure this was the move that the Lord wanted for us, although he questioned how he could reach two hundred thousand people? That was beyond what he could imagine; and he can imagine a lot!

Personally, I was not sad at all to be leaving Davenport. I was so excited and couldn't wait to get to a bigger city with more than one shopping mall! The kids were older and I could sense that I was moving into a whole new season; a new beginning. I couldn't get to Phoenix fast enough, even though it was the hottest place that I'd ever been to in my life!

I went with Tommy to take an early look at the church on 3rd St, and the city of Phoenix. My first impression of Phoenix was good, and I liked it despite the heat, as it was so much bigger than Davenport. At the motel, I thought it would be a good idea to do some laundry while we relaxed by the pool, enjoying the beautiful sunshine. A short while later, we noticed that the whole area leading out of the laundry, and down to the pool, was completely filled with bubbles. After asking me how much laundry soap I used, Tommy was horrified when I told him that I had put in a whole container of Ivory liquid! We were so embarrassed. So, pretending that we had nothing to do with it, we sneaked quietly off to our room. We waited until everyone left the pool area before going back to get our clothes out of the machine. Good one Marja!

Jo Lummer drove with our family to Phoenix, while her husband Paul stayed behind with their two boys, to tie up some loose ends. We stopped over at Tommy's uncle's house in Texas on the way through to Arizona. While we were there, we decided to make a trip or two across to Mexico to pick up some items for our new home. On the way back into the United States, Tommy asked me where my "green card" was. I told him that I had packed it in the moving van, which was probably already in Phoenix.

Tommy knew that this could cause a problem, so he told me to let him do all the talking when we reached the border. He was driving; I was next to him, and Jo was by the passenger door. Kristie, Luke and Matthew were in the back seat, which they shared with some of the items that we had purchased, including a very large, colorful, ceramic giraffe. The border guard asked Tommy some routine questions, such as where was he from...where was he going...etc. After he had answered his questions, the man looked directly at me and asked, "Where are you from?" Tommy answered for me saying, "She is from Davenport, Iowa." The border guard ignored him and continued to look straight at me and said, "I'm not asking you, sir, I'm asking the lady sitting next to you." At that, my heart started to pound in my chest. Pointing to myself, and in my strong Swedish accent, I said innocently, "Who, me?" Of course, that gave me away instantly. When I couldn't produce my "green card," the officer abruptly told me to get out of the car and go with him.

All I could think of as I walked off were Tommy's words earlier as we had approached the border crossing, "Because you don't have your green card, you could be put in jail." I was so afraid that he might be right. Tommy told Jo, "I don't know how long this is going to take, but please take care of the kids." By this time, all three of the kids were crying... really crying, believing that their mother was surely going to jail.

They finally released us two hours later, after satisfying all of their questions. They issued me a permit so that we could return the next day to finish our shopping. It had been a traumatic time for everyone. One of the questions that the border patrol had asked us the day before was, "What do you have in the trunk?" Tommy had answered, amongst other items, "just dirty clothes."

The next day while walking along holding Jo's hand, Matthew looked up at her with his little crossed eyes and asked, "Jo, would Paul have told that man that he had dirty clothes in the trunk?" She knelt down and said "yes." It had obviously been troubling him that his father had revealed his dirty laundry to a stranger so freely! He was so cute and innocent, and I was relieved that the extent of the trauma he had suffered was so small.

As the years went by, we saw no reason to change my citizenship, deciding that it would be easier to apply for a green card, allowing me permanent residency. Tommy has fun telling people that he's married to an "alien," the term given to foreigners like me by the Immigration and Naturalization Services. I do still have a strong Swedish accent, am a Swedish citizen and hold a Swedish passport, but I am an American at heart.

The kids were eleven, ten and five when we arrived in Phoenix in 1979. We bought a house in a cul-de-sac at 54th St and Thunderbird. I set about getting our house in order, while Tommy settled into his new job.

Jo helped the ladies in the church office get things set up the way that Tommy liked. She played an important role in helping Tommy make a smooth transition into our new church. Unfortunately, things didn't work out for her husband Paul in Phoenix. After only a few weeks, Jo moved back to Davenport to join him and continued working for the various Pastors that followed Tommy at Westside Assembly. I missed her greatly.

Before leaving, Tommy had asked Dale and Lynn Lane over to our house to tell them about the position that he had accepted in Phoenix. He asked Dale to consider moving with us to start a brand new bus ministry at the new church. Both he and Lynn were excited, and shared how they had both sensed that Tommy was about to make a change, but had no idea where he would be going. They had decided in advance that wherever it was, they would be going too. When they heard that our destination was Phoenix, they both laughed as they had just bought a brand new snow blower, after years of using a shovel. They said, "Well, we can blow sand instead!" It was perfect; the Lord had been preparing them for the move also.

Dale and Lynn arrived with their family in February, 1980. It was wonderful to have them here with us.

Lynn happily accepted the position as Tommy's assistant in the light of Jo's return to Iowa, which was perfect, as they had both worked side by side with him in Davenport. Lynn knew everything about him and how he liked things done, so it made sense to secure her as his secretary. Tommy is very particular and with all that he had planned for the new church, he needed someone who could hit the ground running. She certainly filled those shoes and has been "running" with him ever since.

Dale started as the bus director for our church, later

becoming Tommy's right hand man as associate Pastor. During his time with Tommy, Dale wrote a book titled *The Second Man*, which speaks of the importance of being an effective leader in a supporting role, which he has learned and lived. Through the years, Dale and Lynn have proved themselves to be the most loyal, supportive, and loving couple. We count them both as two of the greatest gifts the Lord has given to us; they are like family.

As Tommy's first Sunday in the pulpit loomed, we were both scared, wondering if we had made the right decision, and jokingly toyed with the idea of running away back to Mexico, but knew, of course, that this wasn't an option.

The church was absolutely packed. Everyone came to see their new Pastor, and of course to check out his wife and family. I dressed very conservatively for me, and wore a black suit and high heels. Tommy looked like a monster his first time in the pulpit as one of his eyes had become totally red, bloodshot from the stress of moving. He was nervous at first, but once he got going he was amazing and very captivating. After the service, many in the congregation stayed to offer words of encouragement and gratitude to him for accepting the position as their new pastor. We both felt very comfortable in our new church.

Each week the congregation grew bigger and bigger which really encouraged Tommy, and confirmed to us both that we had made the right move. It grew from two hundred to eight hundred in the first month, and after a few more months, had swelled incredibly to two thousand people.

It was a very exciting time as the Lord seemed to be duplicating what we had in Davenport, but with greater speed and ease. Ministries started to appear as the church caught the vision to win souls, with buses going out on a weekly basis bringing the unsaved to each service in droves.

We quickly recognized the need to move to larger premises, so when the opportunity to sell the 3rd St. building came, we moved to North Phoenix High School. Once there, we experienced capacity crowds and realized that this move was only temporary. Our next move took us to East Phoenix High School, which was now ten miles away from 3rd St.—a long way to expect a city congregation to move. Nevertheless, the services continued to fill up quickly.

Tommy and I appeared on the local TBN television program twice a week. I never felt comfortable being in front of the camera and often felt like an idiot, afraid that people wouldn't understand what I had to say because of my accent. I would sit next to Tommy in fear, thinking, *please don't ask me a question.* How on earth could I have thought that I was movie star material? The Lord obviously knew me better than I knew myself.

A few months after arriving, the deacons of Phoenix First Assembly threw a pool party for us with a Hawaiian theme. The stage was set for the fun loving side of me to come out in full view of all our new friends and surprise my husband as well. I have always been playful and was kidding around with one of the deacons whom I'd just met. Somehow I ended up pushing him into the pool. Talk about spontaneous... Tommy couldn't believe what I'd just done and was upset at first; but as everyone began to laugh, he joined in, seeing the funny side of what had happened. This party seemed to set the tone for our new lives in Phoenix, especially for me. I enjoyed the spirit of the people that we met; there was something light-hearted and adventurous about them.

There was never a dull moment in our house. It was always busy, with five or six boys hanging around at any given time. It seemed to be in a constant state of "chaos." Even so, it was always a home, and exactly the way we wanted it to be; a fun place for the kids to hang out with their friends. I made time to get involved with all the games and antics that the boys liked to do, which gave me the title among the boys' friends of the "coolest mom!" They all called me "Mar." I had so much fun with my boys, and we loved to play cards, shoot hoops, swim, and play hide and seek.

One time, the boys thought it would be fun to cover Larry Kerychuk's house with toilet paper, and so did I. He is a very good friend of Tommy's and lived a few streets away from us. I felt sure that he would see the funny side of having toilet paper all over his house and yard. I was wrong about that one! At church the following Sunday, I saw him standing in front of the boys and they looked scared to death. I had to come clean and tell him that I had been a party to the boys' antics. He looked stunned at first and then burst out laughing. We all laughed. It had been fun, and Larry had been a good sport, but I thought better of what I had done and decided that I would leave the T.P. raids to the kids.

Kristie took a while to make friends in the church, but once she did, she was involved in everything.

In the summer of 1983, Kristie went to Kansas City to spend some time with her grandparents and her cousin Danielle.

Sadly, while she was there, on June 16th, 1983, Tommy's dad, Hershel Barnett, went home to be with the Lord. He had preached a sermon at a Wednesday night service, went home, set his alarm for 5:30 a.m. to play handball, but never woke. Joy realized that something was wrong when he didn't respond to the alarm and woke up to find that he had died sometime during the night.

Tommy was absolutely devastated when he got the news. He left the house and went for a walk, even though it was still dark outside. His dad was his role model, his hero, the man whom he had the utmost love and respect for as a father and a mighty man of God. He had pastored his own church in Kansas City for over forty-three years.

So much of what my husband had initiated at Phoenix First Assembly was inspired by what he had witnessed his dad doing in his own church. His father was a great leader and was gifted with the ability to create innovative, new ways of doing things, and applying them to ministry.

Tommy and his dad had never discussed the eventuality of his death, so Tommy was totally unprepared for it when it came so suddenly. We all flew out to Kansas City, where Tommy performed the funeral service; it was huge, and a great tribute to a great man.

In the time that followed, I watched my husband struggle as he tried to come to terms with the loss of his father and what he had meant to him. The realization that he had built his life and ministry on his father's faith and foundation instead of his own came as a revelation from the Holy Spirit. The assurance that the Holy Spirit had always been with Tommy and would continue to be with him for his every need was a turning point in his ministry. He was entering a new season in his walk with the Lord, a season of first hand revelation and wisdom directly from God.

I had no idea that there had been anything missing from Tommy's prayer life; he always seemed to pray regularly. I didn't realize how strong his father's influence had been on him. Now that he was gone, I saw the anguish in my husband as he struggled to come to terms with his great loss.

He started to pray more, going for hours to the mountains behind the sanctuary. The Lord was forcing him to draw closer to him. He was teaching Tommy an important lesson; that firsthand revelations from God are the difference between mediocrity and success. It was a lesson that Tommy needed to learn to enable him to reach the heights the Lord had planned for him in the coming years.

It was a tough time in both our lives, and as Tommy learned how to live without his father, I was about to embark on a journey which would lead me closer to my mother, whom I barely knew.

In 1984, Kristie and I went to Finland to visit my birth mother. For years we kept in touch through letters, but for some reason, I now felt the urge to see her in person. I had written her a letter asking if I could come visit her, and was overjoyed to receive her reply saying that she would love to see me. It had been almost forty years. I was a small child the last time I saw her.

Our reunion was awkward at first. I asked Kristie to pinch me in an attempt to try and release some tears to show some emotion. In my mind I had imagined over and over again how this moment would be. Now that it was finally here; I found I didn't have any feelings toward her at all, which made me feel very sad. It was the strangest feeling, and I wondered if my mother was feeling the same way I was.

As the hours and days passed, slowly, we began to get to know each other and I began to warm towards her. She revealed truth to me in a way that only my mother could. What I had felt was missing in my life, the part of me that yearned to understand who I was, was no longer a mystery to me. During the time that we spent together, she spoke of my father, and her struggles as a young mother alone with a newborn baby. She was also able to express her deep feelings of guilt at sending me away to Sweden at such a young, vulnerable age.

That visit changed both our lives. My mother started down the pathway toward forgiving herself, and I gained new insight into my heritage and who I am. The natural bond between mother and daughter that had been severed so many years before was now mended, and it felt so good! I returned to America, leaving behind all my feelings of insecurity, and taking with me a new sense of confidence in who I am.

In 1985 we opened our new sanctuary on Cave Creek Road, which at the time was on the outskirts of Phoenix. Today however, the city has grown so much that it is considered to be "Central Phoenix." It had been a long, hard road. We had prayed for it, fasted for the money to pay for it, and at last it was done. Tommy had asked the congregation to give their best gift ever; and we had led the way.

After leaving Davenport, we had a residual of thirteen thousand dollars from our house sale. We purchased a small piece of land in the desert, which multiplied to over $350,000 when a Jack Nicklaus Golf Course was planned for that area. Also, when Tommy was young, his parents had given him a mutual fund, with a value of around $8,700. His dad had advised him to never give this trust fund away. It was to be for his retirement as he had signed off on Social Security, which he could do, being a Pastor. Through the years, Tommy had added to the fund, and it was now worth $160,000! We met together as a family and discussed in detail what we should do. My first question was, "Did God tell you to give it?" He didn't answer me, not wanting to influence our decision in any way. We all voted a unanimous "Give it all to God!" And we were not alone.

The response from the congregation was overwhelming as the people gave sacrificially in cash and gifts in kind. They had caught the vision, taken ownership of the project and answered the call.

Tommy was concerned that no one would come out for the dedication of the new sanctuary. He needn't have worried; the sanctuary was completely full; all three levels. Before the service started, he peeked through the side doors to see the sanctuary not just filled, but people were sitting in the aisles. He panicked, and ran back to his office and cried out to the Lord to help him be the preacher that He called him to be.

Until now, Tommy had felt that he was just a country preacher, who had never been to the country. Now the Lord was asking him to be something for which he felt totally unprepared. The Lord calmed his spirit and renewed his confidence with a fresh anointing. He didn't preach the sermon that he had prepared, but the one the Lord gave him in that moment. Its theme was, "The Glory belongs to Him alone." It was awesome!

After the service, I didn't see Tommy for quite a while and wondered what had happened to him. When he got home, he explained how he had been so overwhelmed by God's goodness in bringing us through all the trials of the building program. To finally see the building finished and full of people was almost more than he could bear.

That afternoon, he had taken a drive to our previous church locations in Phoenix and then back up to Cave Creek, all the time reflecting on God's goodness, and thanking him for making it possible. Many people, both rich and poor, had been part of the sacrificial financial giving that was needed to make this beautiful new sanctuary a reality. This was the first of many new buildings that would be built for the glory of God on our seventy-five acre property. This would not be the last time that God would call us to lead the way in financial giving.

Also that same year, we had planned a vacation to Sydney, Australia with Luke and Matthew. Just before leaving, however, I received news that my father in Sweden was very ill. I knew that I had to go to be with him instead of going with Tommy and the boys. I left as soon as I could get the travel arrangements made.

My father hadn't opened his eyes for two weeks. When I saw him I patted him on the cheek and said in Swedish, "It's Marja. I came all the way from America to see you; you have to open your eyes." I held his hand and said, "I know you can't answer me, but I want to tell you about Jesus." As he looked at me, I explained salvation, and shared with him some of the wonderful things that the Lord had done in my life. I said the sinner's prayer and then said to him, "If you understand, squeeze my hand." I felt the pressure as he gently squeezed it, and then he closed his eyes. Two days later he died.

It was an awesome privilege to lead my father to the Lord. What a gift for me and for the man who had spent a huge part of his life devoted to his little girl from Finland. In Sweden, the custom is to keep the body for ten days before the burial, so I wasn't able to stay for the funeral, but I had been there for what counted; someday I'll see him again. As I sat on the plane back to America, I felt a peace and love rise in my heart as the Lord comforted me in my time of loss. Finally, my father knew who God was; now he was with him in heaven. I thanked God for this special time he had given me with him. In 2004, my mother joined him in heaven at the grand old age of 104 years old.

In 1987, it looked like one of Tommy's dreams, to build a modest little prayer chapel, was about to come true. His dream was to have a wonderful desert garden surrounding the place of prayer on the mountainside along with a counseling room with phone lines available for those in need of prayer and help in coping with problems.

He hoped it would be a symbol to the community, as well as a reminder to them of God's presence. He shared his dream with his board, the other pastors, and the people of the church. Monetary gifts began pouring in... from the rich and the very poor.

At that time, and unbeknownst to Tommy, the city of Phoenix coincidentally decided to condemn eleven acres of the church's property right where the prayer chapel was to be erected turning it into a part of the Phoenix Mountain Preserve.

With exaggerated lies and distortions, the local newspaper, environmentalists, and Satan-worshippers blasted the church's plans before the community. Naturally, the citizens of Phoenix became alarmed envisioning an ostentatious seventy foot, lit-up prayer tower spoiling the beautiful, natural landscape. What else were they supposed to think? This was exactly how the media had presented our prayer chapel to them.

Tommy was devastated by the way the tabloids were shamelessly portraying him as though all he was interested in was money. It was such an injustice, and I felt so sorry for him. It was very difficult for me to see him in so much pain. He was crushed, hurt and very angry at the press, especially when he saw the ridiculous cartoons that they were releasing. He had tried to do his best to create something that would be a blessing, but had been completely misunderstood and misrepresented. He called the newspapers to try to get them to retract the stories, telling them that they had published stories that were wrong and deceptive, but they refused to do so.

During this time, he was very hard to live with, making our home a very tense place for the family. It took him a very long time to get over it, but he never let it affect his preaching. I admired him for the way he never missed a beat, despite how he was feeling inside. He knew that the only way to get through this was to take his pain to the Lord in prayer, and that's just what he did.

Sadly, the church withdrew its request to build, stating that it was not the intention of the pastor or the church to hurt anyone, but rather to help the hurting people of the community. Tommy continued steadfastly to believe that no one can thwart God's plans. "For I know the plans I have for you, declares the Lord, plans to prosper you and not to harm you, plans to give you hope and a future" (Jeremiah 29:11, NIV). He surrendered his dream to the Lord, knowing that someday, a prayer chapel, for God's glory, would be a reality.

Life settled down, and little did I know at the time, but I was about to realize a dream of my own; to further rebuild my broken relationship with my birth mother. Since my visit to Finland eight years earlier, my birth mother had been talking about how much she wanted to come to the United States to see me and the children, and meet Tommy. In 1992, she finally came with my half sister, AnnaLee, for a visit. I was thrilled!

We had so much fun together and ate more candy and chocolates than I had for a long time. Tommy got quite a shock when he noticed from the pulpit how puffy my face had become, even though he'd seen me all week! It was happy eating; we were just enjoying each others company. They stayed with us in our home, and once again I was the interpreter. I was much better than I had been back in 1965, when we went to visit my family in Sweden. My sister could also speak English quite well which made things a little easier.

Tommy loved my mother and thought she was the sweetest woman he had ever met. They hit it off immediately despite the language difference. He had become pretty good at getting over that barrier after years of experience communicating with me. Oh, how far we had come together! All the trials of our early years together seemed so far behind us now. Praise the Lord!

Before we knew my mom and sister were coming to America, Tommy and I had been invited to Dr. Don & Ann Bogue's daughter's wedding. I wanted to go, but didn't want to leave my family at home alone, so we decided to take them with us. We all had a wonderful time together. I was so glad we did, as they had never experienced anything so beautiful before.

While they were here, we took them to "Rawhide" in Scottsdale since they'd never seen what the old southwest was like, except on television; it was interesting and fun to see, even for me. There were so many places I wanted them to visit in a relatively short time. My friend Joann and I took AnnaLee to Las Vegas to see Tom Jones in concert. It was just great to be sharing so many new experiences with them; I didn't realize how much I had missed being with them.

Before they left to go back to Finland, both my mother and my sister attended a Sunday morning service at our church with me. I can't describe how it felt to have them by my side, in this great church, with my husband preaching from the pulpit. I was overwhelmed with gratitude to the Lord. When Tommy gave the altar call, they both went forward and gave their lives to the Lord. It was a special moment that I will never forget, and one which I will treasure for the rest of my life. It was a special moment for Tommy also. The Lord had given him a unique opportunity to reach back a generation into my family, and lead them to the Lord.

Back at our house, my mother pulled me aside and spoke the most loving words to me. She told me of how much she had loved my father and how he was the kindest man she'd ever known. She shared how, from the moment we were separated, she had missed me more than she could ever express with words, and had never stopped loving me. I was her firstborn, and my place in her heart never had, and never could, be taken by anyone else. This trip sealed our love for one another, and completed a work that had started years before during my first visit to Finland. The Lord had made me whole. My mother has always loved me; I no longer feel insecure. I am Marja Kaarina Barnett.

Timing is Everything

The Lord took the dreams that Tommy laid down years before, and brought them back greater than he could ever have imagined.

In 1993, a dream that Tommy had held in his heart for almost forty years became a reality with the opening of the Los Angeles International Dream Center. As a young man, the Lord had laid a vision on his heart while he was driving through the streets of Los Angeles; that someday he would pastor a church in this great city. Matthew had received a similar vision to the one that had been placed in his father's heart years earlier, but now, just as it had been for Solomon, it was time for the son to fulfill it.

It began with the urging of the Assemblies of God for Tommy to respond to the need for an inner city church in L.A. I wasn't sure why they were asking my husband. He was busier than he had ever been in his life and the last thing he needed was another responsibility. Still, I knew he had felt a calling to Los Angeles for many years, and thought perhaps the Lord was going to finally bring clarity to his vision.

Tommy met with a top official from the Assemblies of God denomination, who eagerly informed him of why they thought he was the man for the job. He emphasized the great need for a new kind of church in the inner city of Los Angeles, one which would reach out into the community, and not wait for the community to come to it. A church that would make a difference and an impact unlike any church had before. The Assemblies of God believed that if anyone could do it, Tommy could. He listened carefully, and didn't make any commitment, but assured him that he would pray about it.

As much as he tried to push it aside, he couldn't get Los Angeles out of his mind; it was time to finally answer the call. He called the official and told him he would take a look at it and get back to them with his decision. Matthew asked his father if he could go with him to LA to see the church. It was the old Bethel Temple building, which was famous for being one of the first Assemblies of God churches birthed after the Azuza Street revival.

It had long since lost it glory, and was now right in the middle of gang-infested Los Angeles, with a dwindling congregation of twenty-six. The minute they entered the building, Matthew knew this was his church. He never said a word to his father; thinking surely he would never consider him to pastor this innovative new work. Nevertheless, he held it in his heart, knowing that if it was God, it would happen.

On their return to Phoenix, we met as a family to

hear Tommy's report, knowing that if he decided to take it on, it would affect us all. He felt confident that he could handle the responsibility of being the founder and spokesman nationwide, but not the everyday responsibilities of the pastor. We were concerned that the burden would be too great for him to bear on top of everything else he had on his plate, but he assured us that it would be okay, if he could just find the right person to be the pastor.

Over the next few months, Tommy contacted the top ten evangelists who had preached at our church; each of whom he believed could do the job. Each one of them was excited at the prospect of being part of such an innovative new work, but once they saw the building, where it was situated and realized the enormity of the undertaking, one by one, they all declined. Faced with the dilemma of having to find someone to pastor this new church, Tommy did what he always does when he doesn't know what to do; he prayed.

It was during one of our regular early morning Monday prayer times that a good friend of his, Craig Smith, approached him and said, "Pastor, I know that you are looking for someone to pastor the LA church, and I've been in prayer about it. This might sound strange, but I feel that your son needs to pastor the church." Tommy was caught off guard, not expecting to hear this, but listened as he continued to share, "I know he is young, but I know for sure that the Lord wants you to know, that your son can pastor that church." No one knew it, but Tommy had been thinking about Matthew for a while; this was the confirmation that he needed; Matthew was the man for the job.

When he told Matthew of his decision, Matthew was excited and scared all at once. He was only twenty years old and had no ministry experience. Part of him couldn't believe that he was being asked, even though he had always dreamed of having a church that would be open twenty-four hours a day. Years earlier, he had told his father of this dream on one of their many Sunday nights out after church. He couldn't understand why hospitals and convenience stores were open 24/7, and yet churches were only open on Sundays? What if someone needed help in the middle of the night? It was a good question, but one that Tommy didn't have an answer to all those years ago. But now it was different. The timing was right for Matthew's vision to become a reality.

The first few years were extremely tough on my young son, and on us as a family. Matthew was forced to rely on the Lord for everything, which is just how the Lord wanted it to be; this was a new work and he didn't want him to rely on what he had seen working at Phoenix First Assembly. After all, his mission field was the inner city of Los Angeles, not suburban Phoenix.

Some of the things that we do at Phoenix First, like the adopt-a-block ministry, feeding the hungry and clothing the homeless, did work in Los Angeles. However, Matthew felt there was a need to go one step further, to provide housing and discipleship training for them all as well. There were some great people that caught his vision for the community, who came alongside him to help with the huge undertaking of building relationships, discipling people, and restoring their faith in God. I had asked the Lord to send people to help my son, and he had.

Matthew's philosophy to reach people was to place himself in another man's world and begin to love what they love. He got out into the surrounding neighborhood and began to learn their languages. He became interested in the sports that the Hispanic community loved, and learned about their holidays and celebrated them in his church. His goal was simple: to show them how much they mattered to God, that he cared about them, and so did Matthew.

Matthew's diligence, personal approach and new way of doing things, started to pay off and the church began to grow. It soon became apparent that the church was not going to be able to accommodate the growth that was happening; he would need to find a new home for the L.A. Dream Center. He had heard that the old Queen of Angels Hospital was up for sale and decided to take a look at it. After taking a tour of the building by himself, he called his father, excited about what he had seen and eager for him to come and see it also.

When Tommy saw it on his next visit, he became just as excited as Matthew. Dilapidated as it was, they could both see the reality of their vision come to life in this huge four hundred thousand square foot building! They shared with each other visions of what ministries could be on each floor and dreamed together. It had been abandoned for many years and would take millions of dollars to restore. It could be done; but it would take a miracle!

It seems that when faith-filled people like my husband and son mention the word miracle, it gets the Lord's attention. The building was initially priced at $16 million, but we were able to purchase it for $3.9 million with $500,000 down: just the miracle we needed.

After purchasing the building, Tommy began traveling during the week around the country, and the world. For eighteen months, he shared the vision of the Dream Center with everyone, preaching and receiving honorariums that went directly to help support the Dream Center financially. It was very tiring for him, but he was motivated by the incredible miracles that were happening daily, in the lives of the lost and hurting who now called the Dream Center home.

Now, fourteen years later, he still leaves immediately after our Wednesday night service, catching the 8:06 PM flight to Los Angeles, to spend his day off at the Dream Center. However, he tries to never miss a Sunday service at our church in Phoenix.

It was a big adjustment for me, getting used to Tommy being away from home so much on a regular basis, but after awhile I began to enjoy my time alone. Eventually we both learned to appreciate our precious time together.

A while back, we invested in a property in Flagstaff that Tommy dreamed of retiring to one day. It was right on a golf course. We would go to Flagstaff every Thursday on his days off and I could handle the short stays, but could never picture myself living there in my old age! It was all paid for, but this dream was not to be. There would be no thoughts of retirement for my husband, not for awhile anyway.

We decided to sell the Flagstaff property and buy an

apartment in central L.A. so we would have a place to stay when we went there each week. I was happy. I'd always thought that it would have been so boring sitting around with a bunch of old people talking and playing golf. After all, I am a city girl. Real estate in Los Angeles is so ridiculously overpriced, and the only way we could get in the market was to buy an apartment on the 14th floor of a building right on a fault line!

Not long after we had bought our apartment, there was an earthquake. Earlier, on the day of the earthquake, I had been shopping at a mall in downtown L.A. and had a mild panic attack. I took some pills to calm myself down, which made me really drowsy. When the earthquake hit, it made our whole building sway. Tommy was scared that the building was going to fall down and tried to wake me up, but I was so relaxed and out of it, that he wasn't able to get me to realize the gravity of what was happening. I'm sure it was the Lord protecting me, as I don't think I would have handled it well at all!

In 1997, on his 60th birthday, Tommy decided to run from Phoenix to Los Angeles to raise money for the Dream Center. He thought it would be a great way to commemorate his birthday and raise money to keep his dream alive at the same time. I thought it was a great idea; we both love a challenge. I decided to run part of the way with him. My son-in-law, Kent, sponsored me $10,000 for 100 miles, but I ended up completing 150 miles before deciding that I'd had enough. My toenails started to come off and I thought "forget about that!"

It took Tommy twenty-one days to run the 422 miles, which was the equivalent of running a full marathon every day, in a row, for three weeks. It was really hard on his body and he also lost many of his toenails, had huge blisters, and his feet swelled two sizes bigger than normal... but he did it! I joined him in downtown L.A. and we ran the last seven miles together. It felt great! Per mile pledges totaled nearly three quarters of a million dollars; his effort had single-handedly allowed the Dream Center to continue renovations and remain open.

Back when we were in Davenport, Tommy had dreamed of someday preaching to ten thousand people each week, which was about ten percent of Davenport's population at the time. The Lord has brought his one hundredfold blessings on Tommy's earlier dream and more. Today, Tommy reaches millions of people each week through the Dream Center's weekly television program, more than he could have ever imagined back in Davenport.

God is faithful to His Word. When Tommy and Matthew were contemplating going to Los Angeles all those years ago, the Lord told them that if they would reach the people that nobody else wanted, he would give them the people everybody wanted. The Dream Center is a testimony of the Lord's work and is as diverse as you could imagine, with the homeless sitting alongside movie stars and wealthy business people in any given service.

Matthew continues to mature in the Lord and gain insight on how to fine tune and develop more ministries to suit the city and community that he is serving. He is loved and respected as the pastor of "The Church That Never Sleeps."

Tommy and I celebrated our twentieth anniversary

of pastoring Phoenix First Assembly in 1999. It was an amazing milestone in our ministry, and I could hardly believe that all those years had passed. It was a special time of reflection for us as a couple as we gave thanks for all that the Lord has accomplished through us. Tommy had always wanted to fly on the Concorde, so the church surprised us with a trip across the Atlantic, something we may never have experienced if it had not been for the generosity of our congregation.

In 2002, I ran the L.A. marathon. I trained for a whole year in preparation for the run, and at the last minute, Kristie decided to join me, even though she hadn't trained for it at all. We got separated during the run and I had no idea how she was doing; I just had to carry on without her. There were 444 people registered in my age group and I finished at number 34! It was quite an accomplishment.

I found out later that Kristie had almost given up, but had seen Nancy Hinkle along the way, who cheered her on, telling her that I was not too far ahead of her. As she had not planned to do the run, all Kristie had to wear were fashionable high cut shoes, totally wrong for a marathon. At the end, she was exhausted and in a lot of pain. She left immediately after finishing the marathon, without rehydrating herself or having anything to eat, and was still wearing the same clothes she had run in! She got on a plane and headed back to Phoenix.

During the flight she fainted on the way to the bathroom, and when she came to, she told the attendants that she had just run the L.A. marathon. They couldn't believe that she was traveling so soon after such a huge run! When they landed, no one was permitted to leave the plane, and there were paramedics called on board; it was a huge drama. She was in pain for a couple of weeks and ended up getting thrombosis. She definitely has the unstoppable Barnett spirit, believing that anything is possible!

Back in 1996, Tommy's niece, Danielle, won the "Miss Kansas" competition, and was the first runner up to Miss USA. In 2005, she won *Survivor: Guatemala*, and Tommy wasted no time in creating an entire illustrated sermon service around the survivor concept, showcasing some of the great survivors in the Kingdom of God. Danielle made a guest appearance to the delight of our congregation, we were all very proud of her.

Tommy celebrated his 50th anniversary of preaching the gospel in 2003. It was a very humbling experience to have all those years of ministry remembered and "paraded" before us as our church honored Tommy and our family. We have so much for which to be grateful.

When you're in the thick of *doing* the Lord's work, there is very little time to appreciate the fruits of your labor. Our church, however, is great at giving God the glory, and taking the time to recognize what the Lord is doing on a weekly basis. There is not a Sunday that goes by that Tommy doesn't remind us to "never take this for granted; there are not many churches where hundreds of people flock to the altar to receive Jesus every Sunday." Phoenix First Assembly is an amazing place; it truly is "the church with a heart."

We found out what kind of heart our church truly has when in 2005, our grandson Chase, suffered a severe head injury while vacationing with his cousins in Payson, Arizona. Kristie called me, hysterical with the news that he had fallen off the back of a 4x4, landing on his head! Shocked, I began to cry, at which she responded, "Let me talk to Dad!" I was crying and praying all the way to the hospital, and seeing the helicopter, which had brought him to Phoenix landing, almost sent me into a state of panic!

The whole family was at the hospital, along with some close friends. When I first saw him, my heart sank and all I could do was cry and pray. Chase has the Barnett spirit; charismatic, and a bit of a rascal, which made it even harder for us to see him lying lifeless, and unconscious on the hospital bed. Tommy handled the situation well, although I could see the stress on his face throughout the whole ordeal.

There was a church and nationwide call to prayer. "And we know that in all things God works for the good of those who love Him, who have been called according to His purpose"(Romans 8:28, NIV). There were a lot of people fitting this description petitioning the throne room of heaven during this time on Chase's behalf, so we knew everything was going to be okay. We were overwhelmed by the response of our congregation to rally behind us as we all exercised our faith together, asking God to heal our grandson.

God was merciful. Chase was healed completely, with only a few scars on his head as evidence of the events that had almost taken his life. We stood on God's word, and once again, he had come through for us. I am so thankful to the Lord for the many people who make up our congregation, and are always there when we need them.

Dream Centers, following the model exemplified in Los Angeles, have sprouted up all over the United States, and around the world. Our very own "Church on the Street" ministry, after which the original template of the Dream Center in L.A. was fashioned, finally came into its own in 2006. One of the biggest challenges over the years has been to find suitable, affordable housing in downtown Phoenix, to accommodate the hundreds of men and women, who find refuge and hope within our program, after being in prison or living on the streets.

For years, we have housed the hurting and the homeless in small houses scattered around the downtown area of Phoenix. Finally in 2006, the timing was perfect to change the way we did things. After many hours spent looking for the perfect location, the opportunity presented itself to buy an inner city hotel to house our very own Dream Center.

The hotel would need to be renovated, but would not be as huge an undertaking as the L.A. Dream Center had been! Knowing the challenges that our faithful pastors, Walt and Louene Rattray, have overcome through the years, made the reality of finally owning our own building even sweeter. It was well worth the wait!

We held our Sunday night service in the huge courtyard of the former hotel to celebrate the opening of the "Phoenix Dream Center." It was a glorious, cool Phoenix evening and quite a sight to see our entire congregation filling the many balconies that surrounded the pool area. I'm certain the architects, builders and former owners of this property would never have imagined it would one day be a place of refuge and hope, which would impact lives for God's glory in years to come!

2007 was a huge year for our family and Phoenix First Assembly. Once again, we had a lot to celebrate and be thankful for.

A huge celebration was planned to commemorate the 30th anniversary of our annual Pastors and Leadership conference. The Pastors' School, as we call it, began back in Davenport, Iowa in response to the huge interest generated by the phenomenal growth of the Westside Assembly of God church. Pastors from around the world came to Davenport to learn more about how our ministry worked. The staff gave tours of the buildings and answered questions, but it quickly became evident that our small staff was not going to be able to keep up with their regular church duties if this continued.

Tommy's answer to the challenge was to set aside

one day on which he would hold training sessions where pastors could learn how to grow their churches. Tommy would teach them everything he had learned, not withholding anything. By the end of the school, everyone would understand his heart for soul-winning and could recite his favorite saying "the method is not sacred, just the message." In fact, he taught them to duplicate biblical principles, not their personalities. He made their goal of reaching their communities, and growing their churches, achievable.

This, like everything else that Tommy put his hand to, experienced phenomenal growth. The first year thirty people attended, with a staggering three hundred in attendance the following year. One day wasn't enough to impart all that there was to learn, so the school was extended to two days, and then eventually it became three.

Each year I watch it grow and grow, and am in awe of how the Lord is able to multiply the small ideas that he gives us, almost to the point where they're beyond recognition. Pastors' School is like that. It's this huge event that seems to cause time to stand still in our church, requiring the entire congregation to participate to make it all happen. From opening homes to visiting pastors, to directing traffic in the parking lots, it's a huge undertaking; but it's all worth it to see lives changed!

We have seen many mighty men and women of God rise to new heights in ministry after attending one of our conferences. Not everyone's dream is to have a megachurch like ours, but the key thing we emphasize is that our teachings are relevant whether you have a church of fifty, or five thousand. It's all good as long as God gets the Glory!

Usually, the final night of Pastors School is a big "Praise Party," which ends with everyone staking their prayer requests on the side of the mountain behind the sanctuary. This year however, to commemorate the 30th anniversary, we wanted to go all out and get the community involved in our celebration. We set an ambitious goal of filling the fifteen thousand seats of the Veteran's Memorial Coliseum, in downtown Phoenix. Every ministry was allocated a section to fill and we reached out to churches in our community to help us reach our goal.

It was an incredible night and a fitting celebration for thirty years of impacting Leaders for the glory of God. The coliseum was packed to capacity and all who attended knew they were witnessing a night that would go down in history; especially for Phoenix First Assembly. Special guests included, Bishop TD Jakes, Joyce Meyer, and Brian Houston, who all spoke, and Darlene Zschech, who opened the ceremonies singing, "Shout to the Lord." Tommy and I were blown away by the whole night and the amount of effort put forth to make this special evening a success.

It's all about timing—God's perfect timing. In February, 2007, our beautiful, award-winning Prayer Pavilion opened for the first time during our annual Pastors School. The Lord took the dream that Tommy laid down twenty years earlier, and brought it back, greater than he could ever have imagined. It stands on the side of the mountain, a reality, and a testimony to God's greatness and promise.

By design, it's intended to represent a lantern, and

with its glow of changing colors at night, is a cherished reminder that "a light set on a hill cannot be hid" (Matthew 5:14, NIV). It has become a sanctuary of peace from which miracles flow, and the light that symbolizes the Gospel that flows from our campus to the entire valley, and far beyond.

From the moment you step onto the beautiful, landscaped grounds surrounding the Prayer Pavilion, you are struck by a sense of purpose in its design. The walkways are deliberately long, allowing a time of heart preparation as you approach. The elements of fire and water are represented beneath a huge iron cross, providing a place of tranquility, peace and reflection. The huge bronzed doors at the entry of the pavilion itself, resembling two pages of a book, were intentionally designed with no handles on the outside, so that each person would touch the Lord's prayer inscribed on them upon entry.

Not only is it a place of prayer for Christians of all denominations, but more amazingly, is the impact that it has had on the secular community at large. The Prayer Pavilion has won numerous design awards, and was recently nominated for the award of most attractive campus in Arizona, along with eighteen other famous buildings such as the Chapel of the Holy Cross in Sedona, the Mission Church in Tucson and the Whitehouse Ruins in Navajo country.

At Phoenix First, our goal is not to win awards or gain recognition when designing buildings or developing programs. We have found however, they are an inevitable consequence, when your motivation is to do everything with excellence for the Lord in order to win souls.

Our Sunday night service, "Sunday after Dark," is designed to look and feel more like a concert than a church service, so it's no wonder eighty percent of the people that attend are under the age of thirty! "Sunday after Dark" was listed by a local magazine, as one of the top twenty Phoenix hotspots to go on Sunday nights. When a secular magazine, promotes a church as a preferred destination alongside bars, nightclubs and restaurants, *that's* the Lord!

On October 4th, 2007 Tommy turned seventy years old. Our church prepared a fantastic day of celebration which was full of surprises, which started with a rented stretch Hummer picking up all of our family for the service. I could get used to this kind of service! Upon arrival, standing on either side of a huge 10' x 250' red carpet, stretching the entire length of the walkway to the church, people representing the local police, firemen and the armed services greeted us. There were balloons and music, a real fanfare!

From outside the church, we heard the sound of cheering and music coming from inside the sanctuary, and as we entered it was almost deafening. As you may have gathered by now, our church does nothing in small measures. Everything, whether it's an outreach service or a celebration of some kind, is done with excellence to glorify God!

This was no different. We watched as Tommy was honored through gifts of praise from some of his best friends and family, but primarily from the church who loves him. As our family stood on the platform, Tommy began to try and express what the morning's events had meant to him.

Between the tears, he began by saying "I've always wondered what people would say at my funeral. I don't think it can get any better than this!" He thanked the church, honored the board and his team of pastors, and then in true Tommy fashion, began to honor his God, ending with an altar call. It's a rare occasion for him to end any meeting without an altar call; he never wants to miss an opportunity to lead the lost into the Kingdom of God.

Afterwards we had lunch at Kristie's beautiful home with all our family and friends, some of whom we hadn't seen for many years. Matthew and Caroline didn't come to our celebration in Phoenix, instead having their own party for him, in true "Dream Center style." It was also incredible, and just like our children, not any better than the other, just unique to them.

Girlfriends

The Lord was placing women around me whom I could trust... women He knew would make an awesome team... a team that would help me to reach hurting women in a way that had never been tried in ministry before.

Many times over the years, I would find myself stuck, going through the motions of living life, feeling all alone, with seemingly no one I could trust to talk to. Who could understand what my life was like and know the challenges I faced living with such a high-powered man like Tommy? Of course I loved him, but sometimes I just needed to vent and let things out! I would go to the Lord in prayer, and he always gave me insight into what I was feeling; but I still needed friends.

I often found myself wondering, *How do I find a friend?* Slowly I realized that I didn't have to be concerned. The Lord is the best judge of character, and only he knows what both my new friends, and I, needed. I trusted God to choose my friends for me and have found that the key is listening to him, which is why it is so important to build a strong relationship with the Lord as your "best friend." He gives me discernment concerning whom I let in and with whom I share things.

Tommy always says, "If you want friends, show yourself friendly." Simple really, but sometimes we just don't seem to understand, that who we are, is who we attract. The qualities that I believe are important in a friend are loyalty, a good listener, a good confidant and a faithful prayer partner. I have tried to live my life following these principles, and have found that my friends have some, if not all of these qualities, also.

Even so, I had to be very careful what I shared with even my closest friends; some things are better left unsaid, period. I understood my responsibility to my husband first and foremost, and that always took precedence over any feelings I had. My role as a wife and mother was to guard my family, and I knew that this had to start with how I guarded my own words. It has not always been easy to hold my peace, but in hindsight, it has always been advantageous for my family.

Phoenix is where I started to become involved with ministry at a whole new level. Up until this point in my life, the only volunteer activities I had been involved in were helping with make up and costumes for special events back in Davenport. However, the Lord had a new level of ministry prepared for me in Phoenix. What I now realize is that the Lord was bringing women into my life that I could trust, and women who would make an awesome team to accomplish the various ministry events that I would be part of.

At church one Sunday I met my good friend, Joann

Denman and discovered that she lived near me, where we had recently moved, in Moon Valley. We began walking several nights a week. My dog Dutchess, kept a good pace and we worked hard. After our workout, we always felt deserving of a little treat! Frozen yogurt was our favorite. One night we walked *all* the way to get the frozen yogurt and realized we had no money! JoAnn was prepared to walk home empty handed, but not me. I looked at her and said, "Let's ask if we could buy on credit?" She was hesitant, but I was never afraid to ask and so we left with our tasty treat! You should know we did return with money the next day! We took our frozen yogurt and sat on the curb talking. We shared our lives with each other during those walks and over the years we have laughed, cried and of course solved all the world's problems!

Joann opened the door for me to meet many of her close friends, who quickly became my friends, also. Debbie Valentine, Faithe Tines and Mary Ann Hopkins joined us on our walks and we spent many hours talking, laughing and just getting to know each other. It was a great way to fellowship, get out of the house and keep fit in the process. My friend, Dori Grantham, was a door greeter when she and I first met. I invited her to workout with me and the other ladies. I have always enjoyed working out and love to keep fit. Encouraging others and sharing the benefits of living a healthy, balanced lifestyle comes naturally to me because I truly believe that our bodies are God's temple. We should do everything we can to keep ourselves fit for our King.

"Do you not know that your body is a temple of the Holy Spirit, who is in you, whom you have received from

God? You are not your own; you were bought at a price. Therefore honor God with your body" (1 Corinthians 6:19–20, NIV).

We had quite a group; some walking and others preferring to work out in the gym, but all having fun doing so.

One of Joann's friends, Marge Simpson, held a weekly Bible study in her home that I started going to. She was so energetic and friendly.

It was at one of these Bible studies that I met Nancy Hinkle for the first time. We were sitting across from each other in the living room and both noticed a lady coming into the room wearing a huge bow in her hair! It looked so cute on her, but for some reason, this struck us both as being extremely funny. Our eyes met, got big, and we burst out laughing. We've been laughing together ever since. Nancy has the most frank, comical way of putting things and I am always in stitches when I'm with her. She'll say such random things to me when I least expect them. One time when we were out shopping together at the mall, it was over 110 degrees outside. She said, gritting her teeth in a gruff whisper, "this place is so hot, I don't think even the Devil lives here!" Not a true statement, but funny nevertheless!

I loved to invite people to church, and did it all the time, wherever I was. In the mid 1980's, I worked at Dillards, four hours a day, as a fragrance model. I would go to different stores modeling and spraying fragrances on customers. One day, a very stylish lady, around seventy-five or eighty years old, came over to me to try one of the fragrances that I was modeling. I had seen her in the store before and she always looked so beautiful. After telling her so, we started to chat. I told her that my husband was the pastor at Phoenix First Assembly and she said, "Oh, I go there." I asked where she sat and she replied, "At the back." The following week we had lunch and discovered that we had a lot in common.

From that time on, every Saturday, Marge Atkins and

I met to have lunch and go shopping, which would often last from 12–6:00 p.m. Every Sunday, I would sit with her in the back of the church and we would fellowship together. She attended our church faithfully for nearly twenty years, and for the twelve that I knew her, she was my close friend. She died in 1999, leaving a huge sadness in my heart for the longest time. I loved her like a mother. She was a very special lady and a dear friend, and I miss her even now.

Occasionally, I spoke at the "Woman's Aglow" meetings, sharing my testimony. It was at one of these meetings that I met Sharon Henning. She waited behind to talk to me after everyone had gone, and we started chatting. I asked her if she had a home church and she responded, "Why?" I told her that my husband was the pastor of Phoenix First Assembly and he was the best preacher in the whole wide world. I insisted that she come to church with me, so she did.

One day, Tommy patted Sharon on the back and asked her if she'd go and fill up some of the wheelchair buses for Pastors' school, and said, "Just do it until we find someone else." She started as a volunteer, and week after week, Tommy continued to say, "I haven't found anyone yet, just keep up the good work." That was in 1984. Twenty-four years later, Sharon is on staff as the pastor of the special needs ministry with our church, serving and caring for the people who can't take care of themselves. They have priority seating at Phoenix First Assembly; right on the front row, where they should be. Many of them are Tommy's greatest encouragers during the services, freely shouting their "Amen" in agreement with his sermons.

"Fashion Share" has been by far my biggest personal ministry achievement to date. The concept was simple; to create an event through which the women of our church could provide clothing, shoes and accessories for women less fortunate than themselves. For years my friends helped me stage this annual fall event at our church for the homeless women who rode the buses, and any women in need. On the day of the event, all the hallways around the sanctuary would be packed with all the items that we had collected, all sorted into sizes, and then the women would "shop" for free. It was awesome!

There was so much to do, and we had to recruit as many women as possible to make it happen. It was a huge undertaking which required rooms to be set up to receive clothes and many volunteers to repair items, get donations, hair and make up coupons; anything that we could get to bless the women and make each one's day memorable. We'd start collecting clothing months before the event, which came mainly from the women of our church.

In 1990, I was introduced to Judy Rhodes and Jeri Watson by our mutual friend, Mary Ann Hopkins. Judy and Jeri are sisters who own a local store, called "A Second Look." It's one of the largest consignment stores in the United States. After sharing the heart and vision behind the event with them, they began to get excited and saw how they could be of immediate help to us. Many of the clothes that were brought into their store didn't meet their standards for resale and were donated to local ministries; these items were a huge blessing to our women.

Judy & Jeri partnered with us for many years, helping "Fashion Share" to reach more women than we ever could have on our own.

After a few years, we created a mini version of the "Fashion Share" at Pastors' school, which was more of a fashion show and luncheon for the pastors' wives. Six years ago, Masters Commission took the ladies luncheon at Pastors' School to a whole new level, creating shows, resembling those seen on Broadway, instead of a fashion show. It was magnificent and was well received by all as a positive step in a new and exciting direction.

Next year, the ladies luncheon will take on yet another new direction. Exactly what that will look like is still to be determined. All I know is that it will be fantastic; the Lord is never short of creative ideas, and we are never short of women willing to serve other women.

From the Author:

As Marja shared her life stories, and some of the fun times that she had spent with her closest friends, I knew the book wouldn't be complete without hearing what her girlfriends had to say about her. Marja is such a humble woman, and without their voice, we would miss the opportunity to see what a truly beautiful servant heart she really has.

To Marja, with love from your "Girlfriends"

I have not known Marja for twenty years as so many of her friends have. In fact, it has only been two. One day God showed me how much he loves me by giving me a beautiful precious gift. It was Marja. Since that day I have come to know the extraordinary woman of God that she is!

Her love is unconditional through the good, the bad, and the ugly. When circumstances in life try to take me down, as it does everyone at one time or another, she is always there for me. She is there to pray, encourage, and give me hope. I've never known a more generous, compassionate, caring person. When anyone needs her she is there, no matter what!

My favorite attribute of Marja is her ability to be totally crazy and funny. I have laughed more with her than anyone I know. The Bible says, "A merry heart doeth good like a medicine." (Proverbs 17:22, KJV) Laughter is healing to our body, soul and spirit. I have experienced that healing many times just laughing with her.

Marja has made a profound impact on my life and I thank God everyday for bringing us together. Today I am humbled and honored to say Marja is my dear friend. I cherish her and love her with my whole heart.

Deanna Clark

When I was asked to write something about my friend Marja, I thought to myself, where do I begin? There are so many things I could share. Maybe the best place to start is at the beginning.

My husband and I moved to Phoenix in 1986. I was asked to be a part of a Mother's Day fashion show. I met Marja when I arrived at church for a practice. Marja was alone in the hallway waiting for practice to begin. She came right up to me and said "Hello, I am Marja Barnett, the pastor's wife. How do you like these jeans? I just lost enough weight to fit into them!" Her remark was so cute and spontaneous, I was caught off guard. I had never met a pastor's wife that would admit to thinking like me! I mean who isn't trying to fit into their favorite pair of jeans! I thought, *what a real individual.* It was so refreshing to meet someone who wasn't afraid to be herself; even with someone she just met.

Little did I know that this was the beginning of a lifelong friendship. Marja and I not only played together, but we worked together. I can remember one year during Fashion Share. We just finished a rehearsal that was nothing short of disastrous. Tired, hungry, and ready to run away and hide, we slumped down on a bench to commiserate at our friend's bridal shop. Our arms were full of wedding gowns for our show the next day, when we noticed a police car pulling into the parking lot. Did I mention it was 2 o'clock in the morning? How are we going to explain this? We aren't the owners and it is 2:00 a.m.! We were shaking in our boots! Could this day get any worse? You will be pleased to know that we were not arrested! We must have very innocent faces. Somehow, our bad day and long to do list did not seem as overwhelming. We completed our list and Fashion Share was a blessing to all who attended. Just one of many instances where having a loyal friend, like Marja, and trust in God can pull you through. We were thankful we didn't run away.

You may look at Marja and think she is just a pretty face, but she is more beautiful on the inside. She is loyal, intelligent, graceful, a good listener, and a clown all rolled up into one! She is full of the love of God, compassionate, and a prayer warrior. She is the kind of friend you don't have to entertain. We can sit and say nothing, or talk for hours. I can be who I am, and she can be who she is, and trust each other with everything. She has been a blessing to my life and I am thankful that we call each other friends.

Marja, when I think of you I think of Proverbs

"A friend loveth at all times" (Proverbs 17:17, KJV)

That scripture says it all. I am excited to see what the next twenty years of friendship has in store! I love you.

JoAnn Denman

It all happened so fast... an incredible trip with Mom and Dad, our two young boys, and two of their cousins to my brother's ranch home in Idaho. Two weeks of nine cousins sharing the ranch together! Fun, theme parks, swimming, spending the night on the big boat, fishing, eating our "catch," riding the 4-wheelers, target practice, and family fun, food, and frolic. On our way home, after four hours on the road, we were in a serious accident—a tumbling van, people ejected from the vehicle—broken bones, emergency vehicles, hospitalization in Montana, and miraculously, no deaths. Statistics show that it is highly unusual if there are no deaths in a roll over accident. While there were serious injuries, God miraculously spared all of our lives and healed us completely of major injuries. That's where Marja comes in.

For three years earlier, I had been overseeing Fashion Share annually at Phoenix First Assembly, a community outreach for women and teen girls—a day of fun, food, fashion, sharing God's love in word and deed, followed by the world's largest free shopping spree for the needy. That's where I first became acquainted more one on one with Marja and her heart for the less fortunate.

Marja worked closely on the fashion show, helping oversee the selection of clothing for the models. She selected from the thousands of items that had been donated to put together a beautiful fashion show, while ministering God's love to hurting women. Marja was so much fun! She brought God's love to others by being "real," showing and expressing care in everyday ways. She is quick-witted and funny, and helped us all laugh so many times, but she has a deep heart of concern for others who are hurting. Out of her own pain and the journey to her personal healing, she has become a mighty vessel of love and light for the Kingdom of God.

Back to the accident. When I was in ongoing physical therapy for my broken pelvis, tailbone, leg and shoulder injuries, and more, I decided that in my overcoming, I would set a goal to run in the 5K Run for Life for the local Crisis Pregnancy Centers. Being a champion of overcomers, I asked Marja if she would join me in the run in just five months. She responded with a quick, "Of course, I would love to do that with you." I was thrilled. Having a partner would help me push through.

We worked out together, and she was patient, waiting until I got stronger and stronger. One day, I had rehearsal for the Christmas Production, so we decided we better get some miles in, so we met at the church to go around and around the huge parking lot before rehearsal. Little did I realize that my hips would be greatly affected in the healing process by the uphill and downhill, pull and strain. In just a few days, I couldn't move. As I went back to therapy, they said, you've strained the muscles around the healing bone area, and will probably have to skip your run. I said, "No, cannot do that." So my therapist, said, "Okay, we have treadmills onsite and I am restricting your exercise off the pavement back to the treadmill, where there is less pounding." So, I called Marja… and she said, "No problem. I'll just come to therapy with you, and we'll do our run on the treadmill that day. All is fine, I'm here for you, to support you, and help you as you regain your strength." That was more than fifteen years ago.

For twenty-five years, we've shared the joys and struggles of life, along with worship services, gatherings and fun experiences together with many other women. What a privilege it is to know this very special woman of God who lives and loves freely—from the inside out. She is a tough soldier in the Army of God, in a woman's skin.

Sue Gaub

When you read this book, you will be amazed by the life of this wonderful woman, Marja Barnett. She is nothing less than outstanding in all that she does for the Lord, her family and her friends. She has been my special friend for over twenty years.

From the first time we met, I was drawn to her sweet, humble qualities. She has been there for me through some very hard times, always listening, encouraging and praying for me. I have my very own cheerleader in Marja. When she says, "You can do it Dori!" I really believe that I can, because she believes in me.

Marja is so energetic and so much fun to be around, she's always thinking of new ways to have a good time. God has truly blessed her for her unwavering faith in him. She is truly the Proverbs 31 woman...except, she can't sew!

She is such a genuine, loving, caring woman; she makes me a better person, just being with her. Some friendships are for a season, but my friendship with my beautiful friend is for a lifetime..."Now let's go shopping!" I love you girlfriend.

Dori Grantham

Time is very valuable. Marja always took time to spend with me when I needed her most. She has a very tender heart for people and on our first meeting seemed to be drawn to me with a purpose; as if she knew that I needed a church. I felt an immediate connection with her. Her words to me that day were from the Lord, as I had been struggling to find a church since accepting the Lord seven years earlier. At the time, I was attending a Lutheran church, and here she was encouraging me to try Phoenix First because her husband was a wonderful preacher.

The church on Cave Creek opened in February of 1985 and my husband and I attended. We sensed this incredible love. The building was full, and the Spirit of the Lord was awesome. Then Pastor Barnett said to come back on Sunday Night and on Wednesday Night. We looked at each other as we had not attended that many services in a week, ever! Our lives have been completely changed since then, starting us on an incredible journey that has led to God's purpose for our life.

She is always concerned about the needs of people, and over the years has visited the special people that I minister to, and spent many hours encouraging and loving them.

She has a very open heart to love and it pours out of her to others, and increases as she gives it away. Marja has the heart of a giver. Once, I admired the earrings she was wearing and she gave them to me! Marja is beautiful inside and out.

Sharon Henning

Wow, what can I say about my friend Marja Barnett? A lot!

Generous Spirit: Marja is generous in every area of her life; with her love, time, heart, prayer and money. In some of the hardest times of my life, she has been there for me with a prayer, an encouraging word and an understanding heart.

Encourager: Marja will encourage you and really make you think that you can do anything! She has encouraged me to step out in areas I never would have tried, only to see it was the very hand of God nudging me on.

Friend: "A friend loves at all times." (Proverbs 17:17, NIV) Marja is not just a fair weather friend, she is there for others whatever they are going through. She is full of mercy, but not afraid to tell you if you're going the wrong direction.

Servant: She is not so proud that she won't roll her sleeves up and help in any area that's needed. She's vacuumed the church! She still picks other women up for church and keeps those that are house bound company. Nor is she too proud to love, touch and pray for the "unlovely" people that are on the streets or come on the bus to our church.

Witness: She tells everyone about Jesus and invites them to church! She always gets the most people to anything; especially to events we have at church! Marja loves God and loves others.

Fun: We have so much fun together. She is as serious about life as she is about God, but she knows how to have fun. We have laughed until our stomach's hurt. Most times when we go shopping people want to know why we are so happy and full of joy. They always think we are sisters, not because we look alike! But, because we are so free with each other.

I have traveled this nation in full time ministry for thirty-four years and Marja is the first "Pastor's Wife" I've known that truly knew, accepted, embraced and loved the position God has called her to. She's the "best" girlfriend!

Nancy Hinkle

Marja was the first real friend I had when we moved to Phoenix from the Bay Area. I will never forget the moment we met at a Christmas coffee in 1988. We discovered that we were neighbors and shared a passion to walk. That was the beginning of many late night "prayer walks". She walked through my husband's near-death with me, and a disappointing move to New Mexico after a wonderful "good-bye" party at her house—she threw me in the pool. We had many "prayer calls" over the miles apart and trips to Los Angeles in the beginning days of the Dream Center. I laughed with her, and cried with her at some of her "firsts": birth of a grandchild, seeing her children's dreams come true. I loved all the Swedish accents when I met her family from afar. I loved the times we had with Joy Barnett. She truly embraced me as a sister; I felt like family. Marja encouraged me to speak publicly, and gave me confidence that I had something to share. There were moments only God knew how we got there: lost keys, shopping charades, and oh how I loved to clean her closet. I always gleaned a fabulous find! Better than all the laughter, late nights and prayer hikes. I truly discovered a woman who feared the Lord. She is to be praised—a rare jewel not purchased or obtained. Thank you for those wonderful, faith-filled excursions we had; I feel young at heart just remembering.

Mary Ann Hopkins

Marja is my hero, I love this lady. In February, 2007, I marked thirty-five years of working for her husband; half his life! Marja and I have always respected each other and have never had a harsh word or bad spirit towards one another in all the years that we have been friends. She is happy to be his wife, and I am happy to be his secretary; it's a perfect relationship for all. I am touched when Marja says that we are like family, because I know she is a woman of her word. She is a grand lady and I am proud to call her "friend."

She's always *glamorous*! Like the time in Davenport when Dale and I drove by their house on a Saturday, and there was Marja.... out in her yard cutting the grass. Not like anyone else you have ever seen running a lawn-mower! Picture this—a glamorous Swedish lady, long denim skirt, cute little top, colorful bandana on her head, walking like she was on a runway with her tall, cork, wedge shoes. I love this woman!

Lynn Lane

We all have people that come into our lives. Some to me are acquaintances, some casual friends, some what I consider close friends and then there are those special people who become "treasured friends." Marja and I have developed that kind of treasured friendship. No matter how much time passes between our visits, the value of our friendship never changes. It's a friendship that doesn't require that we be together often, but when we do have the chance to get together over a cup of coffee, lunch, etc., it's as though time stood still between our visits. We have enjoyed just being friends and knowing we can be real with each other.

I have watched her as she struggled with her role as a "pastor's wife,," admiring how she handled criticism that came her way, holding her head high and knowing her role and place as the wife of a highly visible man. There were times that the role became very hard for her, and some of those times she would call me and we would talk it out.

Yes, my friend Marja is a very normal gal... with tender feelings, a sympathetic heart, a genuine love for people, and overall a very strong woman. I have always said that Marja was designed for a definite purpose, and that being, the lady who stands "beside" a very visible and public man... a man who holds the highest calling: "A servant of God."

Jo Lummer

I am so privileged to be one of Marja's friends. It has been an amazing pleasure doing girlfriend things together. She is so much fun, and is the "I Love Lucy" of the girlfriend world. She never takes herself too seriously, and is the life of any get together. She is always the center of cute pranks we play on one another. She is great fun to travel with, she just goes with the flow without ever insisting on her own agenda. But more than all the fun, she is a compassionate listener and caring soul, always willing to pray, give aid, and above all, give love.

Judy Rhodes

My first encounter with Marja was around fifteen years ago when I moved to Phoenix. I started attending PFA and was introduced to Marja through a friend. *Wow...* was my first exclamation! Not only was a beautiful, blonde, fashionable woman standing in front of me, but when she spoke, she immediately made you feel so comfortable and welcomed.

As time went on I found myself continually being encouraged by her. Whether it was working out together, attending women's gatherings, shopping, or having lunch, she always had the kindest of words to speak that elevated one's self-esteem.

When I took ill, Marja was the first to come visit me at the hospital bringing her love, concern, kind words, prayers and humor. Yes, humor, this woman puts the fun in funny. Working with her at the annual ladies luncheon at Pastor's School has always been a high honor for me. Even when I felt she could always get someone else to do the job she always reminded me that she wanted me. Though our times together are not as many because of busy schedules, our friendship picks up where it left off. After all these years she continues to make everyone feel so very special. She truly has been a bright light in my life. I'm so very grateful for her.

Marge Simpson

In 1985 we came from Canada to Phoenix, Arizona and started attending PFA. What a delight it was to meet the Pastor's wife, Marja. When we were introduced, this gorgeous blonde extended a warm "no walls, non-intimidating" welcome. I liked her right away! In the years that followed, our friendship allowed us to have a lot of fun and laughter as well as face some serious challenges.

While helping her at the ticket sales table for the Pastors' School ladies luncheon, I would watch as hundreds of ladies would line up. They would be excited to meet Pastor Tommy's wife and with that same warm "no walls, non-intimidating" welcome this gorgeous blonde would make them laugh, make them feel important, and just happy to be there.

One day Marja asked if I would do hospital visitation with her. All the true and sincere Godly attributes that I had witnessed in her life became even more evident. I would meet her at the church and excitedly she would just jump into the car with a list of people that we were to visit that day. As she entered their room and introduced herself their face would light up and as she prayed for them with such love and compassion a spirit of peace would comfort them.

Marja never hesitates to boldly tell people about Jesus and invite them to come to PFA because as she says it, "The Pastor is the best in the world. He's my husband, you know." Her sense of humor, and the absence of negativity, ungratefulness, competition or self-pity, always creates an uplifting atmosphere that you just love to be in.

She has proved to be a loyal unchanging friend. During some very dark and troubled times in my own life she has given me such great support, encouragement and wise "common sense" counsel. Her transparency and vulnerability is a badge of honor she can wear proudly. She is extremely generous, never holding tightly to, or collecting "things," preferring "people." Her life speaks loudly the language of kindness—you know, that language that the deaf can hear and the blind can read.

What a lady! What a model she has been to me. Her character shows off God's craftsmanship. The light she has held up has beckoned me to follow, and her beauty marks are not just a memory, but they leave an indelible mark on my heart.

Faithe Tines

Marja and I have been friends for about twenty-one years. Fourteen years ago we became related when her son Luke, married my daughter, Angel. Today we are still good friends!

Several things I love about Marja are that she is very

generous, appreciative, funny, full of life, fashionable and *very* competitive.

On one of their family visits to Lake Couer d'Alene someone suggested swimming a mile from the island to our cabin. Marja met the challenge head on and made it! Angel was only fifteen years old and the swim just about killed her!

We have had fun trips to L.A. with the girls and I have many stories about the fun times we have had together, but none that should be revealed in her book! One thing I will say, and Marja will understand is: ummm…

Donna Unicume

I was introduced to Marja by our mutual friend Joann, twenty-three years ago.

At that time we all helped with makeup for the Christmas production at Phoenix First, applying some very bright makeup! This is when I found out that we all lived close to each other, and that Marja liked to walk. As often as we could, we walked up some very steep hills, with Marja always leading and pushing us to work harder!

It was on one of these walks I got to really know her heart. At first I was intimidated just because she was the "Pastors Wife," but I was pleasantly surprised to discover how real Marja is. She is beautiful on the outside, but it's her Godly qualities on the inside that make her the very special person she is to so many of her Girlfriends! She is a true inspiration to me.

What qualities make her a standout?

Sense of humor

Uplifting

Prayer warrior

Encourager

Righteous woman of God

It has been a blessing and privilege to call Marja my Girlfriend!

"There is a friend that sticketh closer than a brother [or sister]" (Proverbs 18:24, KJV).

Debbie Valentine

I am blessed with friends who love me for who I am; friends who understand the challenges and parameters of my life, and know that they all have a special place in my heart. All of my friends are wonderful gifts from the Lord; to be loved and treasured as God's best for me. God has never let me down, or led me astray, and has chosen the most wonderful friends for me. They're all different and unique; and we're all designed to be just right for each other!

My tribute to Kristie

In closing this chapter, I would like to say a special word about my daughter Kristie. She has become one of my closest friends and a great confidant. There are things that I can't tell Tommy, my boys, or even my closest friends; but I can tell Kristie. Every Friday, on her day off, we go to lunch, shop, or just hang out together. I never take for granted the fact that she takes her day off to spend time with me. She always has time for me and is just like her dad; a great encourager. I have watched her grow into a beautiful young woman, flourishing in ministry in her own right. I value our friendship, in some ways more than that of our mother/daughter relationship. I love her more each day and am so proud of her; she epitomizes the word "girlfriend."

The Fruit of Faithfulness

All three of my children have faced adversity of one kind or another, but they all kept going. Tommy always says, "You can think about quitting, because you know that you're not going to! Barnetts are not quitters!"

The relationships I have with my children are all different, none better than the other, all unique between each one of them and me. I was always there for them when they came home from school; they knew they could count on me. When the kids left home, I thought I would feel bad, but I never got time to notice they were gone, as they were always at the house. We had the best of both worlds, getting to see them, without all the work.

Tommy's relationship with them was different to mine because of his demanding schedule. Even so, he always made time for them, in the ways that counted to them.

When she turned sixteen, Tommy surprised Kristie

by renting a limousine to take her on a date to an elegant restaurant, making her feel like the most special girl in the world. She ran track, which is Tommy's favorite sport, and they would get up early and run together around Paradise Valley Mall before school. He would always go to watch her train, while sitting in the bleachers practicing his sermon for Wednesday night.

When Luke was very young, he showed an interest in playing golf. Tommy mowed and maintained a two hole, golf course on our property, which was on a five acre block, just so he and Luke could play at their leisure. When Luke was nine years old, twice a week, he and his father would get up at 5:30 a.m. and play nine holes of golf before Tommy headed off to work, many times dressing on the way there!

Matthew's "special time" with his dad was spent at Whataburger on Sunday nights after church. He would wait patiently for Tommy to finish talking with people after church, knowing that his time would soon come, and they would be alone together to talk. Matthew *loves* to talk, and would often exhaust us with his seemingly never ending questions. Tommy always made it a priority to spend this time with Matthew; no matter how tired he felt.

Tommy understood each one's "love language." He did what his father had done with him; spent time doing things that counted to Tommy, not himself. There were so many things that he did with the kids to show them how much he loved them, like going to the boys' Little League games or wrestling matches, or taking Kristie shopping. He made sure that whatever was important to them became important to him.

The Fruit of Faithfulness

Kristie graduated from high school in 1986. Over the years, she had told us many times that she had no desire to pursue a college education. All she wanted to do was follow my example; to be a good mom and be home with her kids. The realization that Kristie had seen the value of growing up with a mother who was always there for her, and wanted that for her own family, was incredibly humbling to me.

Even though we always knew that Kristie would make a great wife and mother, when she first told us that she was dating a boy in the church named Kent, Tommy was not happy. He had the reputation of the "bad boy" and was not who he saw his "princess" being with at all. I quickly became the mediator between Kristie, Kent and her father. I tried to help him realize that he could either accept her choice or risk losing her for good. They were both very young, and there was no stopping them: they were in love. Kristie and Kent were married on July 8th, 1988.

Our first grandchild, Kent Jr., was born the following year. It was such an exciting time in my life; to be a grandmother for the first time. I'll never forget being at the hospital, waiting on his arrival, surrounded by friends and family; all just as excited as I was.

Chantelle, our first granddaughter, was born just over a year later, on August 4th, 1990. And then, along came her son, Chase, on March 4th, 1992. With her family complete, Kristie devoted herself to caring for her husband, her home and her children. Her main focus was her family, although she continued to help out with some of the big events at church, sometimes flying as an angel or roller skating in the Christmas pageant.

In the early years of their marriage, they went through some rocky times, and Kristie endured many years of hardship and sadness on her own. She never let us know how tough things really were for her, until one night over dinner, when she poured her heart out to her father and me. We were devastated to hear that she had been so unhappy, carrying this burden alone for so long.

It was the first time I ever fasted in my life. I drank only water and juice for three days and became very weak and anemic, but I truly believe that the Lord honored my sacrifice as I saw their marriage slowly being restored, better than it had ever been. I have always been so proud of the way Kristie stuck with her marriage through all the trials. She understood, as I had in the early years of my own marriage, that there was a greater purpose for her marriage than her feelings could possibly reveal to her. They had made a covenant with God together; honoring him was what really mattered.

Kent had run his own division of his family's pest control business since the age of nineteen. When they were first married, they both worked really hard to make it grow, but like so many businesses, it was too small to hire employees, forcing Kent to do all the work himself. To fulfill their contracts, Kristie would often drive him to his jobs at night as he was already exhausted from a full day of work. She answered phones, kept up with the bills and looked after the kids for nearly five years.

Finally, their hard work began to pay off and the business was able to sustain itself, enabling them to hire people to relieve Kristie from her daily duties. Just recently she reminded me of a lunch date, when she was only thirteen years old, with her grandmother Joy. During their lunch, they had studied a document hanging near their table detailing the history of the restaurant they were in. She made the comment to her grandmother, "Someday I want to build a company like this." She and Kent are well on their way to doing just that. Today Sexton Pest Control is a thriving business with over one hundred employees.

Investing in People

An attitude of service and a positive outlook have brought Kent Sexton success.

BY KAZ LEON

Kent and Kristie Sexton
Occupation: Owner, Sexton Pest Control
Words of Encouragement: Proverbs is filled with wisdom for living and success in business.

I am so grateful for my wonderful son-in-law Kent, whom I love as a son. He is an awesome husband and father, a great man of God and an outstanding blessing to our church. He lives to be a giver; that's his ministry; to be prosperous and help advance the Kingdom of God financially. I am so glad that all those years ago, Tommy and I didn't get in God's way by standing in the way of their relationship. Only he knew the potential that was waiting to be released in Kent, and that he was destined to play a pivotal role in our family and his kingdom.

For many years, Kristie had no aspirations for herself other than being the best mom that she could be. She was very happy with her life and had no desire to be in the ministry. God, however, had a different plan waiting to unfold.

In 2004, Kristie and her friend Lisa went to Sydney, Australia to attend the Hillsong Women's Conference. It was life changing. During this conference the Lord birthed in her a vision for the ladies of Phoenix First Assembly, "Passion in the House." Tommy named her ministry "Phoenix Girls" and Kristie was launched on a ministry path and she has never looked back. As a volunteer, Kristie developed Phoenix Girls from a monthly gathering of ladies of all ages to a weekly Bible study, annual conference and monthly "Unleashed" ladies night out.

In 2005, Kristie became a full time staff member as Pastor of Servant Leaders for Phoenix First Assembly. She lifted the area of "volunteers" or "servant leaders" as we now call them, to a whole new level. Her goal is to get the people of the church more involved and productive by making it as easy as possible for them to get connected with one of the 220 ministries within the church. In addition to this full time position, she runs our APEX program, speaks regularly at our church, and travels the world preaching, all while remaining a devoted wife and mother. She is *amazing*!

Kristie learned the secret that eludes so many women; the number one priority must be your family. Putting them first allowed her husband to be successful in his business and her children to grow up in a secure, loving home. Only then did God call her to her pre-destined place in ministry.

Luke finished high school with no dreams of being in ministry at all. His dream was to become a professional golfer and he was extremely talented, playing in many pro events. One day Tommy planted a seed with him, saying that even though his heart was with golf, he should keep his mind open to preaching one day, if the opportunity arose. Two weeks later, Luke got the opportunity to speak at a local church that didn't even know who Tommy was. He remembered his dad's words and agreed to the engagement. He borrowed one of Tommy's sermons and nervously stumbled his way through the message. He had seen his dad give the call to salvation many times before, so when the time came to give the altar call, it came naturally. A lady came forward in response to the call. This was the turning point in Luke's life.

From this point on, Luke embraced every opportunity to preach, speaking locally and often spending the summer with his grandmother in Kansas City, speaking at churches that she scheduled on his behalf.

Luke and Angel had a rocky start to their relationship, although Angel admits to falling in love with Luke the moment she saw him, when she was just sixteen years old. They dated and spent most of their free time together and one summer she invited him to go with her and her family to their lake house in Idaho. Luke's excitement at the prospect of spending more time with her quickly turned to confusion when Angel acted with indifference toward him during his stay. Things got worse when Luke retaliated with the "cold shoulder," and the situation escalated into a complete breakdown when Angel said that she would rather kiss one of her horses than him. They broke up and went their separate ways for a while, but Luke always knew that she was the one for him; one day they would be together again.

Luke continued to speak regularly and was excited when his first opportunity came to speak at Phoenix First. The week before Luke was scheduled to speak, Tommy asked him to come to his car to hear something. He played a tape of a woman singing and asked him, "Do you know who this is?" Luke replied, "No." Tommy said that it was Angel and that her father Ed had talked to him about whether Luke was interested in dating her or not, as she had expressed interest in dating him. Tommy added, jokingly, "If you're not interested, I'll get Matt; one of my boys is going to date her!" My husband the matchmaker!

The night that Luke was to preach at Phoenix First, Angel was also scheduled to sing a solo. After the service, they went out on a date, and that was it; three months later he proposed, and six months later they were married.

The Fruit of Faithfulness

For two and a half years they traveled as evangelists throughout the United States and all over the world. In 1995, Luke received a call about a pastoral position with a church in Dayton, Ohio, which was struggling under the leadership of their 78-year-old Pastor of forty years. Luke agreed to take on the challenge to rebuild the church, and upon arrival set about doing all the things that he had seen his father successfully implement to win souls over the years at Phoenix First.

The church began to grow and things seemed to be going well, until the old Pastor, who had not been in agreement with the change of leadership, started to cause problems from within the congregation. The previous pastor owned the church building and one Sunday, Luke and the congregation of six hundred people, arrived to find the church doors locked and police everywhere.

It was a traumatic time for both Luke and Angel as they struggled to make sense of all that was happening to them. Luke called us, distraught and seeking advice on how he should handle the situation. We felt so helpless and distanced from them. I felt like immediately flying over to comfort him. I felt so sorry for him, but all we could do was listen, try to help them gain perspective, and pray. After much deliberation they decided they would start afresh, and "Beaver Creek First Assembly" was born.

They held temporary meetings at the local Holiday Inn and eventually bought an old building and created two sanctuaries, twenty thousand and seven thousand square feet each. The cost of the project was $2 million which was raised by the small congregation of four hundred faithful people that had followed them. It became one of the top ten churches in just over three years.

Late in 1999, Luke accepted an invitation to Pastor the "First Family Church" in Whittier, California, stepping into the shoes of the seventy year old Pastor that had shepherded them for thirty-seven years. He led the traditional church through a huge, long overdue transition, forming ministries with a focus on community outreach. This rocked the boat of the predominantly white congregation, as the surrounding community was seventy percent Hispanic. That's what happens when you do a good job of reaching out into the community: they come!

There was a huge migration out of the church, but in spite of this, the church grew from four hundred to one thousand, two hundred members in seven years. The church struggled to recover financially as the incomes were lower. Nevertheless, the church did eventually prosper. They paid off all their debt, transformed their community and everything started to run smoothly again. It was around this time that the Lord began speaking to Luke about a change that he was getting ready to make in his life. He began to feel unsettled and restless, and after a lot of prayer, and without telling his dad, he resigned from the church.

Luke had received offers to move and pastor other churches every year, during the seven years he had been in Whittier. Now that he had resigned, there was not a single offer on the horizon. His resignation left his family with no income, making it a very scary time for them, but he knew it was what God had asked him to do. He was to take this huge leap of faith and trust him.

When Tommy heard the news, he couldn't believe it! He didn't understand why he would do such a thing, and questioned Luke, asking if he still wanted to be in the ministry. He said that he did, and asked us to support him in his decision. Not long after he received the news, Tommy asked him to consider working with him here in Phoenix. He had been contemplating starting an emerging leadership network, based at the Phoenix Dream Center, and thought Luke would be able to help him develop the idea. Luke agreed and not long after, moved his family to Phoenix.

This was the first time that Tommy had worked with Luke and was pleasantly surprised at the skills Luke displayed that he never knew he possessed. He asked Luke if he would help with some staff restructuring; Luke took the challenge head on. Tommy was very impressed with him and actually told him one time, "I can't believe you're my son!" He was process focused and great at analyzing situations and implementing solutions; something our church needed.

At Phoenix First, we have always been great at outreach, but Luke identified the need to develop ways to "inreach" to our church. It quickly became evident that Luke would be a valuable addition to the Phoenix First staff, and in 2006, he became the Pastor of Ministry Development. In the short time that he has been here, Luke has initiated two innovative new programs; Apex and Fusion.

Apex is designed to help the newly saved, and newcomers to Phoenix First to pursue personal growth and align with a church family. We encourage them to build relationships and find out about the many ministries that we have to offer, to see where they fit. Fusion is the name given to our Wednesday night service, which consists of a one hour worship service, followed by small "life group" fellowship on the campus. We have over eighty affinity groups with up to twelve people in each who get together, discuss the night's teaching and do "life" together. In addition to these programs, he has revamped our children's program with "Elevate kids," which has one thousand children and is still growing.

Luke and Angel's first daughter, Aubrey, was born on March 28th, 1998. Their second, AnnaLee, named after my sister, was born on March 30th, 2000. The girls call me "Bling" grandma. I love to watch all my grandchildren getting involved with ministry, and am grateful that we have such outstanding children and youth programs for them to be a part of. They're both beautiful girls, with the sweetest spirits, just like their mom.

The Fruit of Faithfulness

I'm so happy that Luke and Angel are back here with us in Phoenix. All the trials that they faced away from us have allowed them to grow and mature in a way they may not have been able to had they remained here with us. We are now benefiting as a church and a family from the wealth of wisdom and life skills that the Lord imparted to Luke during his time of "training." He's amazing and I'm extremely proud of him!

When Tommy first told me that he was thinking about sending Matthew to pastor the Dream Center in L.A., I couldn't believe what I was hearing. How could he even consider sending my baby away, he was only twenty years old. I was afraid for him; how would he survive in the inner city of Los Angeles, let alone pastor a church? He had no ministry experience, not one day of pastoral duty, and didn't know anything about a church budget or how to run a board meeting.

This was the second time in our marriage that we had not been in agreement about something, and even though Tommy and Matthew both felt he was the best man for the job, I struggled with their decision for a long time. This whole episode caused one of the worst panic attacks I'd had since I was a small child back in Sweden.

Not long after Matthew left Phoenix, Nancy, Dori and I went on a trip to L.A. to combine shopping with a visit to see Matthew. When I saw him, my heart sank. The stress showed in him physically; he had put on a lot of weight, and his face had broken out in pimples. To make matters worse, someone had been killed near his church in a gang-related drive by shooting during his first week of being in L.A., which made me fear for my son even more.

On the way home, I started to get the jitters and by the time I got home, the jitters had progressed into a full blown panic attack. It's a terrible feeling, making you feel like you're going to die. It was so severe that I ended up in the hospital and on medication.

Thankfully, as time went by, God replaced any fears I had with a perfect peace in my heart about Matthew. I know that he is well on his way to accomplishing all that God has planned for him; he is in God's perfect will for his life. I have learned that sometimes God's perfect will for us doesn't look very safe or secure. Matthew persevered through many trials alone, and succeeded against all the odds to make a difference in a community that many have turned their backs on.

The Fruit of Faithfulness

I'm very proud of him, and was so happy when he finally found someone to share his dreams with. Caroline grew up in Los Angeles and coincidentally, is American born of Swedish descent. She and Matthew met at the L.A. Dream Center where she served with the Adopt-a-Block program, going out on the food trucks into the community. She shares Matthew's love for the hurting and the homeless.

When he finally worked up enough courage to ask her out on a date, she was quick to say yes, and it was on that first date that he knew she was the one for him. On one of my trips to L.A., Matthew asked me to go with him and Caroline on a date, which I'm sure she thought, was very strange. Matthew didn't think anything of it, he was more concerned about whether I would like her or not.

We hit it off immediately. It was great having someone to speak with in Swedish. Actually, it was on that date, that I asked her in Swedish, "Will you marry my son?" Matthew asked me what I had said, and I told him to mind his own business.

Caroline answered me, again in Swedish, "Yeah, if he wants me."

I knew then, that it was just a matter of time before we had a new member in our family. Matthew caught her completely by surprise, when he proposed to her at the top of the Empire State building after formulating an intricate plan to get her there. It coincided with a vacation that some of our family had planned, which worked out perfectly, as we were able to celebrate with them after the proposal. They were married on September 10, 1999.

Through Every Season

Their daughter Mia was born on September 4th, 2003, and Caden, our grandson, who will carry on the Barnett name, was born on January 18th, 2006. I don't get to see them as much as my other grandchildren, but when I do, it's always special!

Whenever I go to L.A., Matthew always makes time to spend with me, treating me like a queen! We always have a wonderful time together. The days of tucking Matthew into bed at night, talking about life, his dreams and what he could become, are now just precious memories. Even so, I can't help feeling he will always be my baby; even as I see him forging forward on his quest to change lives for the glory of God!

The Fruit of Faithfulness

I try to never stick my nose in my children's business. The only time I ever felt the need to say anything, was with my boys. They are both a lot like Tommy, in that they *love* sports; any kind of sport. They especially love to play basketball. Knowing firsthand how the combination of sport and the television can consume the peace in a home, I taught the boys to place value on the time they spend with their wives. I encouraged them to set aside a "date" night and to always make time to listen to their wives, even if there was a big game on!

All three of my children have faced adversity of one kind or another, but they all kept going. Tommy always says, "You can think about quitting, because you know that you're not going to! Barnetts are not quitters!"

That's our family motto, and it has, and will continue, to see us through whatever the Lord has in store for us as a family.

Team Barnett

Within the sanctity of marriage, God has blessed us with one of the most powerful dynamic forces in the world. His desire is to give us multiplied blessings and power, unleashed by our hearts unified as one, with one common goal: to glorify him in all we do.

I never like to be caged in, so it was easy for me to give Tommy the freedom that he needed to succeed in ministry. I gave him what I desired for myself; the freedom to be who I am. I have always felt free and fulfilled in my role as a wife and mother, even though I was always at home with the kids, and rarely worked outside of the home.

In recent years however, for the first time in my life, I felt like I was losing my identity. Don't get me wrong. I am thrilled with the way my family excels in every opportunity the Lord presents to them; but learning to surrender them to him has been a real challenge.

Praying for Tommy in ministry is one thing, but

learning to pray for my children in ministry required a whole new level of faith. I felt unsettled and anxious for them as one by one, they became more and more involved in the ministry. This, in turn, presented a new set of challenges for us as a family.

When you love the Lord, and have spent most of your life serving him, it's a natural response, to desire that the Lord use your children in a mighty way for his purpose also.

However, when he answers your prayers and begins to use them, it creates in you a need to rise to a greater level of intimacy with him. You are forced to take your children to the Lord in prayer, realizing that you can't carry the burden alone; you can't be there with them like the Lord can. It is liberating to surrender them to God's care, a step of faith which I try to exercise daily.

The past few years have been challenging for me as I became weakened and frustrated by hormonal changes and continuing women's health issues. Until just recently, I still suffered from an occasional panic attack. Recognizing the risk of depression taking hold of me I've had to fight the temptation to isolate myself from people.

Unbeknownst to me, my volatile state of health was giving my children cause for concern. I didn't want them to worry about me... they have so much on their plates already. One day before the Lord placed the writing of this book on my friend's heart, Matthew flew in from Los Angeles. Concerned that I wasn't doing well emotionally, all three of my kids had arranged a special lunch meeting with me, eager to show how much they loved and cared about me.

We had a wonderful lunch and a great afternoon together... it was a real treat to have all three of them to myself. In between the bouts of laughter and recollections of childhood memories, they expressed their concerns for me, saying, "We just want our mother back!"

I love my family!

There are some things which we need to take control of ourselves and not accept them as "just the way things are." I reached out and asked for help. After some minor surgery and a switch to natural medications, I'm feeling like my old self again!

It can be a vicious cycle, and one which I am learning to cope with by the grace of God. He gives me the peace and strength I need to adjust to changes and bring balance to my life, and he gives me a family to care for and encourage.

As I reflect on what a wonderful husband Tommy has been, it makes me smile. I believe that couples give up on their marriages far too easily. We could have been a statistic, separating early on in our marriage, not giving the Lord a chance to show us what he had in store for us; look what we would have missed!

This year, 2007, Tommy and I have been married forty-two years, and life these days is very peaceful. It's a special place that we have arrived at, almost like a reward for all the years we persevered together. We are best friends now and don't fight at all.

He's my favorite person in the world, my best friend. Sometimes he's like a little kid. I have heard him say many times from the pulpit that the whole church could tell him how great his sermon was, but until he hears it from me, he's not satisfied. It's true!

We always travel to church separately, as he often leaves at 4:00a.m. to pray and prepare himself for the Sunday services. I usually arrive home before him, and when he gets home, he has this little ritual, which is so cute. He will stand in front of me, smiling sheepishly and leaning his head to one side. I know what he is waiting to hear, and it's with sincerity and deep respect, that I give my words of approval and praise to him.

You see, Tommy is more than my husband, he is also my pastor. I was saved under his ministry. Then the Lord gave me the privilege of sharing his life and ministry with him. I believe that I have benefited more than anyone from the many words of inspiration and encouragement that have passed through my husband's lips over the years.

I have learned to leave Tommy alone on Saturday nights, not wanting to get in the way of his preparation time for his services the next day. Instead I pray for him, knowing that this will help him be at his best for the congregation, and for me.

Through him, the Lord has delivered messages to me, intended to help us grow together in Him. The Holy Spirit has been faithful to guide us and keep us safe from harm.

There have been many times when his message has been right on for me... and him. Knowing what is going on in his life, occasionally I will hear him preach a message that I know is ministering to him personally; they're some of his most powerful messages.

Sometimes, he will use our lives, or me, as an example in one of his sermons. I have had people ask if I feel insulted or think Tommy is rude when he talks about me during a service. I always say no; I take it as a compliment. I know that it's his way of acknowledging me, and, I have been known to speak up in my own defense from time to time!

After spending most of our day at church on Sunday, with Tommy usually preaching in all three services, we always look forward to Monday night, as this is our night to spend with our family. We go to Luke or Kristie's house and play games with the kids. I enjoy playing ping pong with Luke, with thirty-two being the most games we ever played!

Tommy still travels a lot during the week, and likes to take me out to dinner when he's home. When we're in L.A., we go shopping together and just hang out, enjoying each other's company. He likes me to go with him as often as I can; it's our retreat.

He always tries to please me, is very generous, and loves to lavish me with gifts. On my 60th birthday, he really went overboard. After celebrating my birthday over lunch, we said goodbye to our family, and drove to a car dealership in Scottsdale. Waiting for me inside was the cutest little Audi convertible with a huge red bow on it. Kristie and the kids had gone on ahead of us and were waiting to surprise me; it was awesome.

I know he loves to buy me things, but what I love the most are the little things he does. The way he always tells me how much he values me, and how, when he walks into the service, he turns to me and tells me how beautiful I look. This always makes my day, as pleasing him, and looking my best are still very important to me.

In the last ten years, I've spent a lot of time at home by myself, but it's different now. Compared to the way I felt during the other seasons of my life; I don't feel alone at all. Now I really enjoy the time that I have by myself, enjoying my quiet times with the Lord. I enjoy listening to classical music, in place of the sports channel which is always on when Tommy's home. He loves football. Actually, he loves sports in general.

I love the way the Lord uses nature to show us how natural and orderly it is for our lives to move from one season to another. The beauty of being able to reflect back on years of a life well lived is that it allows me to see God's perspective of each stage of my life, and the significance of each season. It's encouraging to look back and see God's hand in every situation.

My family is a great source of inspiration to me; we are an awesome team. Each of us has our positions to play, and as competitive as we Barnetts are, we are content to support each other and be the best that we can be together for God. We don't know the future, but we do know the God of the future; that's all that matters.

It is said that a picture can paint a thousand words. My prayer is that my words will paint a thousand pictures in your mind and give you inspiration and vision for your life... the kind of vision that comes through prayer and the knowledge in your heart, that wherever you are, whatever your circumstances, God is with you and desires to give you his perspective and his plan for your life. Allow him to place you where you will glorify him the most and this will answer every desire of your heart to be useful to him. All he is waiting for is for you to trust in him.

Tommy and I ... Just for Fun!
Since our very first day of marriage, Tommy has never hung up his clothes; I always felt like his maid! But in the last five or six years has he started to hang his clothes up, and is so proud of himself; it only took thirty-eight years of training!

His favorite foods are lamb and Indian curry. However, these days, our schedules are so different that he often prepares his own dinner ... in our George Forman Grill.

In our church, it's no secret that he *loves* Starbucks coffee. Every year on his birthday, it has almost become a tradition for the staff and congregation to buy him a Starbucks card; you wouldn't believe how many he receives!

My inability to master the English language constantly challenges me, and has become the source of some embarrassing moments for me over the years. These are a few of my "Marja-isms" as my family calls them.

Instead of ... I say ...

Goose bumps	Chicken skin
Charlie horse	Horse Leg
Birth control pills	Birthday control pills

From the Author:
What a privilege it is to have been trusted to write this incredible life story on Marja's behalf. I love and admire Marja greatly for her steadfast faith in God; she is a true prayer warrior! Throughout the writing of this book, she was an absolute joy to be with, and although recalling her precious life memories was slow at first, she persevered as we pushed through some tough times together. We had so much fun, and considering Marja has a heavy

Swedish accent, and I have a thick New Zealand one, it's quite the accomplishment that I got anything right!

The opening statement of this book, "Behind every great man there is a great woman, and behind them both, is an even greater God" epitomizes the lives of this amazing couple. Too often we see only the finished product, not realizing the work of the master "behind the scenes" of someone's life! In her own words, Marja confesses to knowing she & her husband would not have made it without the Lord's hand on their lives.

First and foremost in our minds while writing this book, was the hope that her experiences would help someone else stay on track and finish their race strong for the Lord, realizing that God's plan alone is sovereign. Jeremiah 29:11 has carried Marja through many difficult situations in her life, and continues to this day.

listen|imagine|view|experience

AUDIO BOOK DOWNLOAD INCLUDED WITH THIS BOOK!

In your hands you hold a complete digital entertainment package. Besides purchasing the paper version of this book, this book includes a free download of the audio version of this book. Simply use the code listed below when visiting our website. Once downloaded to your computer, you can listen to the book through your computer's speakers, burn it to an audio CD or save the file to your portable music device (such as Apple's popular iPod) and listen on the go!

How to get your free audio book digital download:

1. Visit www.tatepublishing.com and click on the e|LIVE logo on the home page.
2. Enter the following coupon code:
   6dcf-657f-f169-3366-a082-3c30-4e5e-8c5f
3. Download the audio book from your e|LIVE digital locker and begin enjoying your new digital entertainment package today!